THE
TOASTMASTERS

INTERNATIONAL® GUIDE TO

SUCCESSFUL
SPEAKING

OVERCOMING YOUR FEARS

WINNING OVER YOUR AUDIENCE

BUILDING YOUR BUSINESS & CAREER

JEFF SLUTSKY MICHAEL AUN

Dearborn
Financial Publishing, Inc.®

Executive Editor: Bobbye Middendorf
Managing Editor: Jack Kiburz
Project Editor: Karen A. Christensen
Cover Design: Scott Rattray, Rattray Design
Interior Design: Lucy Jenkins
Typesetting: Elizabeth Pitts

© 1997 by Jeff Slutsky and Michael Aun

Published by Dearborn Financial Publishing, Inc.®

Printed in the United States of America
97 98 99 10 9 8 7 6 5 4 3 2 1

Library of Congress Cataloging-in-Publication Data

Slutsky, Jeff. 1956–
  The Toastmasters International guide to successful speaking / Jeff Slutsky and Michael Aun.
    p. cm.
  Includes bibliographical references and index.
  ISBN 0-7931-2352-6 (pbk.)
  1. Public speaking.   I. Aun, Michael.   II. Toastmasters International.   III. Title.
  PN4121.S488   1996   96-32584
  808.5′1–dc20   CIP

Dedication

For the most important people in our lives:

My wife, Christine and my sons Cory Michael, Jason Paul
and Christopher Jeremy Aun

My children Amanda Paige and Mitchell Nathan Slutsky

Books by Jeff Slutsky

How to Get Clients

Street Fighter® Marketing

Streetfighting:
Low Cost Advertising & Promotion for Your Business

Street Smart Marketing

Street Smart Tele-Selling

The Toastmasters International® Guide to Successful Speaking
(Michael Aun, coauthor)

Books by Michael Aun

The Great Communicator

Build a Better You—Starting Now (Vol. 5)

Marketing Masters

Contents

*F*oreword

"Mend your speech a little, lest you may mar your fortunes."
—*Shakespeare*

*I*f you are like most people, public speaking is not your favorite task. But in a fast-paced, complex society like ours, which is seemingly ruled by computers, effective verbal communication is vital. We need men and women to inform, persuade, entertain, and inspire. In today's competitive job market, the person with strong communication skills has a clear advantage over tongue-tied colleagues.

Giving a speech can be one of the most nerve-racking experiences known to humankind—and writing one can be just as difficult. So many a potential spellbinder remains glued to his or her seat, daunted by the prospect of facing an audience. But the good news is that jittery nerves, fear of failure, and the procrastination often associated with writing and giving a speech *can* be relieved.

In my years as executive director of the world's leading organization devoted to public speaking and leadership training, I have never met or heard of a "hopeless case." In fact, I could easily fill this book with success stories from formerly tongued-tied Toastmasters who have accomplished what they once thought impossible. I honestly believe that every person who truly wants to become a confident and eloquent public speaker can. Success or failure in this area depends solely on attitude.

So whether you are a novice, scared to death by the thought of facing an audience, or a more seasoned speaker wanting to improve your effectiveness, this book is for you. It offers step-by-step guidance and platform-tested tips that show you how to write an effective speech and deliver it with grace, power, and eloquence. But don't expect to read this book on Sunday and become one of the nation's great orators by Monday. You have to work on accomplishing your goal. Henry Ford once said, "The great trouble today is that there are too many people looking for someone to do something for them." The key to becoming a good speaker is in your hands: Do you have the self-discipline to put into practice the simple rules and techniques outlined in this book?

Fortunately, Toastmasters International® offers a safe, inexpensive, and proven way for you to practice your newfound skills in a supportive environment. Most cities in the United States have several Toastmasters clubs that meet at different times and locations during the week. If you are interested in forming or joining a Toastmasters club in your community or company, call 714-858-8255. For listing of local clubs, call 800-9WE-SPEAK, or write Toastmasters International (P.O. Box 9052, Mission Viejo, California 92688). You can also visit our Web page at http://www.toastmasters.org.

By practicing what you've learned in this book, you don't have to worry about sweaty palms and butterflies the next time you need to brief your coworkers on a new project or chair your second-grader's Halloween party committee. You will feel in control and be persuasive. Above all, you will have gained increased self-confidence from having turned obstacles into personal victory. By practicing self-discipline, you will have learned to control fear instead of letting it control you.

So if you want to become a dynamic speaker, I urge you to do two things: (1) Read this book. (2) Get on your feet and practice what you've learned in a Toastmasters club. Don't worry if you don't sound like a pro at the first attempt. Stay with it, and before long you'll be in command of a skill that can change your life.

Terrence J. McCann, Executive Director,
Toastmasters International
*the world's leading organization
devoted to teaching public speaking skills*

*P*reface

The Toastmasters International® Guide to Successful Speaking will give you the tools you need to become more proficient as a public speaker, which can be critical to your success. Communication is the essence of leadership, so we intend to show you the "what's," "why's," and "how-to's" of effective communication from the platform.

A *London Times* survey, conducted several years ago, concluded that public speaking was *the* most difficult thing for most people to face. Not only was it cited as the most dreaded; it exceeded all other fears combined, including the fear of dying.

Overcoming Your Fear of Public Speaking

This book will provide you with a plan for overcoming your fear of public speaking. Michael Aun's grandfather, Eli Mack, Sr., defined fear as "an absence of knowledge and a lack of information." Most people are afraid to speak in front of a group because they lack the skills and the knowledge they need to present their message properly. This book shows you the techniques and provides suggestions for developing the skills you need so you can address any group with impact and confidence.

Your Speaking Ability Impacts Perceptions of You

The level of your communication skills, whether polished, poetic, or pathetic, causes others to form their opinions about you and your opinions. Their responses often determine whether they buy your product or buy into your beliefs. For a doctor, it may determine whether her patient has enough faith in her surgical skills to be allowed to perform a lifesaving operation. A boss's speaking ability may impact employees' productivity levels. A parent must communicate with a child to guide him or her along an appropriate moral path. Your communication skills can make or break you. Your ability to motivate others is critical to your success in many facets of your life.

Toastmasters International Has Your Plan for Success

While numerous books can tell you "how to" better communicate, all the books in the world are of little or no benefit unless you have a way to plug in and use that information. Several organizations offer programs on becoming a better communicator. Toastmasters International has four major strengths:

1. low cost
2. accessibility
3. progress at your own pace
4. supportive, nonthreatening environment

You'll find Toastmasters clubs located throughout North America and around the world. Over 3 million people have gone through the Toastmasters program. Clubs generally meet weekly. There are currently over 170,000 members of 8,189 clubs located in 55 different countries throughout the world, and the organization is still growing.

Throughout this book, analogies will be drawn from our personal experiences as well as many of our professional speaking colleagues, many who got their starts as public speakers through their local Toastmasters International club. For many people,

Toastmasters International has the edge because the cost to join is minimal, making it accessible for anyone to participate. Meetings generally run one and a half to two hours, depending on the club. Some clubs have "eating meetings" while others offer only coffee and refreshments. Some clubs meet inside an organization and are distinguished as corporate clubs, including IBM, Apple Computers, AT&T, Bank of America, Coca-Cola Co., Disneyland, Eastman Kodak, Hewlett Packard Co., Kraft, Inc., Rockwell International, Levi Strauss & Co., the United States Armed Forces, and hundreds of others.

A typical Toastmasters meeting opens with a brief business session, giving everyone an opportunity to participate in parliamentary procedure, which is a lesson unto itself. A *Table Topics* session is generally next, giving members the opportunity to participate in impromptu speech situations. Generally a topic is presented, and the speaker has two minutes to speak extemporaneously on the subject. For instance, a topic might be: "If I hit the lottery, I'd . . ." The speaker would complete the thought with two minutes of his or her own ideas and comments.

Table Topics are both a lot of fun and challenging. It forces the speaker to think on his or her feet. This ability is one of the most important talents one can develop. It is literally the difference on which some employers promote.

In a time when organizations are "downsizing" or "right sizing," the ability to communicate is the advantage you need. Whether you're an aerospace engineer who is selling an idea or a salesperson who is conveying an idea, the ability to speak extemporaneously is an enormous advantage for you.

Prepared speeches are generally next on a typical Toastmasters club agenda. These speeches are based on topics in the *Communication and Leadership Program* manuals that come out of Toastmasters International World Headquarters in Santa Margarita, California. These manuals are constantly updated and fine-tuned to keep up with the latest challenges facing today's communicator. Following are the first ten speech projects in the initial manual:

1. The Ice Breaker
2. Speak with Sincerity
3. Organize Your Speech
4. Show What You Mean

5. Vocal Variety
6. Work with Words
7. Apply Your Skills
8. Add Impact to Your Speech
9. Persuade with Power
10. Inspire Your Audience

Some of those other topics in the basic manual include the following:

- The Entertaining Speech
- Speech Outlines
- Nervousness: How to Make Your Butterflies Fly in Formation
- Table Topics
- Using Visual Aids
- The Club Meeting
- Meeting Rules and Responsibilities
- Club Leadership
- How To Introduce a Speaker
- Other Learning Opportunities
- Toastmasters Communication and Leadership Tracks

After you have completed the ten projects in the basic manual, a Toastmaster's Club member earns the Competent Toastmaster (CTM) designation. Members may then participate in the Advanced Communication and Leadership Program, working in any of 14 manuals, each with five speech projects. Manuals address career-related topics, such as technical presentation, public relations, and information talks as well as noncareer topics, such as interpersonal communication and storytelling. Upon completion of some projects in the Advanced Communication and Leadership Program, a member can receive additional awards. Those who wish to advance in the ranks of Toastmasters International can also get involved in leadership roles in the local clubs, areas, districts, or regions (e.g., Southeastern United States), and earn one of several leadership awards.

Another aspect of the local weekly club meeting is the evaluation process. Each week, a Master Evaluator evaluates the overall meeting and appoints several Speech Evaluators to evaluate the formal prepared speeches of the week. Toastmasters International provides an evaluation guide in the Advanced Communication and

Leadership Program to help the evaluator assess the strengths and weaknesses of the speaker, based on the goals of that particular speech.

There is also a "grunt" or "ahhh" counter who counts the number of "ahhhs," "ummmms," and "ya-knows" that speakers typically plug into their speech patterns when they cannot think of what to say next. Each weekly meeting also features a "grammarian" to look for grammatical errors.

And no meeting would be complete without a "timer" to keep the speakers on track. One of the principal goals of Toastmasters is to start and end on time. At the conclusion of the meeting, a member gets special recognition for the "Best Table Topic," the "Best Speech," and the "Best Evaluator." Some clubs give traveling trophies and others offer ribbons, but recognition is plentiful.

Toastmasters International clubs also offer various speech competitions throughout the year. Clubs may have a "humorous speech contest," a "tall tales contest," a "table topics" contest, and an "evaluation" contest. Annually each member can participate in the International Speech Contest, which culminates when nine finalists compete at the Toastmasters International Convention held in August of each year in various locations around the world.

Throughout this book, you'll discover dozens of real-life examples about becoming a better speaker, many from some of the top speakers. While the goal of this book is not to help the reader become a professional speaker, many members have gone on to do just that. For more information on Toastmasters International and the National Speakers Association, contact:

Toastmasters International
23182 Arroyo Vista
Rancho Santa Margarita, California 92688
Phone: 714-858-8255
Facsimile: 714-858-1207
For club information: toll-free 800-9WE-SPEAK

National Speakers Association
1500 South Priest Drive
Tempe, Arizona 85281
Phone: 602-968-2552
Facsimile: 602-968-0911

$\mathbf{\mathcal{A}}$cknowledgments

$\mathbf{\mathcal{W}}$e would like to thank Jeff Herman, the best literary agent in the world and a good friend; Ron Specht, a loyal Toastmaster who was responsible for teaming us up on this project; Bobbye Middendorf, our executive editor, and Karen Christensen, our project editor, from Dearborn Financial Publishing, who made us work way too hard to ensure that our readers got the best manuscript draft possible; our friends and colleagues in the National Speakers Association who contributed their insights for this book, many of whom got their start at their own local Toastmasters International club; all the members of Toastmasters International Club 1841, Osceola Toastmasters, Kissimmee, Florida; Debbie Horn, manager of education and club administration for Toastmasters International, who gave us many helpful pointers; and Terrence McCann, executive director of Toastmasters International, who made this book possible and helped us arrange that 20 percent of all authors' royalties earned on the sale of this book are donated directly to the Ralph C. Smedley Memorial Fund.

Chapter 1

*7*alking Your Way to the Top

*7*here is perhaps no greater skill that can help you build your career or business better than effective public speaking. Whether you're speaking to a small committee of ten decision makers or an arena filled with 10,000 future leaders, knowing how to persuasively present your point of view can make the difference between merely surviving or thriving in a vastly competitive environment.

What Kinds of People Benefit from Public Speaking?

What do the following people have in common?: a REALTOR®, a life insurance salesperson, a vice president of finance for a Fortune 500 company, a chiropractor, a nutritionist, a comptroller for a major hotel chain, and a journalist? They, along with Michael Aun, are some of the members of the Toastmasters International Club 1841 in Kissimmee, Florida. They all want to promote their careers or businesses by developing their public speaking skills in a positive environment. Let's take a closer look at several of these members:

Dolores Brown is a REALTOR® who wants to improve her communication skills so that she can deliver speeches to community organizations on how to utilize the services of her company and her profession.

Jim Spinelli, FIC, LUTCF, is a very successful salesperson who sells life insurance and annuity products for the Knights of Columbus. He conducts seminars, called Fraternal Benefits Nights, in his local Knights of Columbus Councils. These seminars focus on the various fraternal benefits and insurance services offered by the Knights of Columbus to their membership.

Jim Smith is vice president of finance for Darden Restaurants and oversees millions of dollars of budgeting each year. He has to sell his ideas to the Board of Directors and his company.

Eric Lerner is a chiropractor who wants the public to know the benefits of his profession and uses his public speaking to spread the word *and* to secure business. In a similar vein, Pam Leonard, a nutritionist who preaches the gospel of good nutrition to her clients, uses public speaking to present her message, her products and her services.

David McKim, the comptroller for Holiday Inns, has to prepare and deliver his ideas to his staff.

Goals of Public Speaking

No matter what you do for a vocation or an avocation, public speaking can be a valuable tool for increasing the level of your success. There are many advantages in becoming an effective public speaker to present your message. Perhaps four of the most obvious, in ascending order of success level, include awareness, understanding, impact and action.

Creating Awareness

Whether you're presenting information on a service, product or a point of view, public speaking provides you with a medium to expose your audiences to the advantages of what you have to offer. Awareness, from a marketing point of view, is the first level of starting to achieve your goals through public speaking. Awareness, in this respect, means a superficial impression, notion or perception about your message.

For example, let's say you're the chairperson for the local children's hospital. Your organization wants members of the community to be aware of the good work they do and to participate in an upcoming fundraiser. To spread the word, you've arranged to make a presentation to several local organizations. As a featured speaker, you first create some awareness for your topic and yourself with fliers that have been mailed along with announcements to their members. So even before you give the speech, you're starting to work toward your goal.

However, you obviously gain most of your audience's awareness during your speech itself. And finally, you might gain a little more awareness via the post-event publicity, if any, that the organizations might do. This could be a follow-up article in their newsletter, for example, that summarizes your key points. So while simply giving a speech can start you on the road to success for your fundraiser, you're not really successful unless you get audience members to take action. In this example, you would achieve success by persuading your audience to participate in the fundraiser. Therefore, it's vital not just to give a speech but to give a *good* speech. If you present your message properly, your potential level of success goes up a notch.

Fostering Understanding

Practically any speech will help create some degree of awareness for the message, but to get a better result from your effort, you want your audience to go beyond a superficial awareness. You want them to understand your message. To do this, you gear that speech to address the needs and wants of your audience. To help your audience achieve a greater understanding, you need to develop and deliver that message with a great skill. The more effective you are in your presentation skills, the greater the chance that your audience will comprehend and remember the key points of your message.

Generating Impact

However, even if your audience members understand your points, they don't necessarily agree with your message. To persuade using public speaking, you must impact your audience.

At this level, you've not only helped your audience to remember your key points, but you've caused them, through your persuasive style and message, to actually "buy into" your message. You want your combined message and style to reach them on an emotional level.

Most people buy (or buy into an idea) based on four basic emotions: mad, sad, glad and scared. You want your message to be so powerful and delivered in such a compelling style that your audience experiences at least one, and preferably more, of these basic emotions.

Most accomplished speakers will use a story or an anecdote to help generate an emotional response from their audience. Some of the most effective anecdotes are from their personal lives and are often about a learning experience or perhaps even a tragedy.

Motivating Your Audience to Take Action

The ultimate result for a public speaker is to combine both the message and the presentation style so effectively that they cause members of the audience to take a suggested course of action. This is certainly the most difficult result to obtain from a speech, but generally it is the ultimate goal a speaker has in mind.

In this book, you will discover a blueprint on how to develop those public speaking skills that create awareness, understanding and impact, and hopefully result in action. You will learn how to overcome obstacles. The most common is to overcome the fear of speaking in front of a group. You'll also need to know how to define your topic, develop the material and fine-tune and effectively deliver your message.

Residual Benefits of Effective Public Speaking

The rewards of mastering your public speaking ability go beyond giving that speech and reaching that particular audience. Some of these additional rewards include increased credibility, increased exposure to your message and increased satisfaction.

Increased Credibility

Public speaking is a form of persuasive communication that literally puts you on a pedestal. Since the vast majority of people in your audience are scared to death to speak in front of a group, they are likely to admire your passion and talent for speaking. Your audience might assume that "if you're speaking on the subject, you must be an expert." You will prove or disprove this assumption by presenting your speech, but in most cases your audience will give you the benefit of the doubt.

Increased Exposure for Your Message

Once you become a prolific speaker on your subject, you will likely discover other opportunities to further present your message through other means. For example, with the credibility your effective speech generates, you might be invited to write an article for that organization's newsletter or journal or your local paper. Some groups might ask your permission to record your presentation and distribute the audiotapes or videotapes to other members who could not attend. If you receive an honorarium for your speeches, recording rights can be an additional revenue stream for you.

A one-hour keynote speech may lead to a half-day seminar at a national or regional convention. You may be asked to participate in a panel discussion or to sit on committees and boards. Public speaking makes you visible, which can lead to other forms of exposure that make you even more visible. This "snowball" effect can put your career or your business on a fast track and give you an edge.

Increased Satisfaction

There is perhaps no greater "high" than that adrenaline rush you get during and immediately after giving a killer speech. You know when you have that audience right where you want them because you're reaching them on an emotional level. You can see it in their eyes. They laugh when they're supposed to laugh. They cry when you make them feel sad. They applaud when they're glad at key points you make. And they nod their approval when you're seeking their support of a critical concept. How can you not love your job if part of your success is getting that kind of immediate feedback from your audience?

With successful public speaking woven into the fabric of your career, you're much more likely to have an easier time dealing with the frays and pilling that crop up in any situation. For example, most professional speakers love what they do. They would rather be in front of an audience more than practically anything else. They also have to spend a great deal of time on airplanes and in hotel rooms. It may sound glamorous, but if you do it several times a week, it gets old real fast. Yet they wouldn't do anything else. You may find that the more you enjoy what you do, the more successful you will become.

Finding the Right Audiences

Every civic club in the world needs speakers for their regular meetings. Organizations such as the Rotary Club, Lions Club, Elks Club, Moose, Jaycees, Sertoma Club, chambers of commerce, Knights of Columbus and countless others offer excellent opportunities for you to let the community know that you are an intelligent, urbane, knowledgeable, responsible, concerned member of your community. You may find other opportunities within your own industry. Think of the credibility you would create by being a featured speaker at your annual or regional convention. While the audience members are probably not your customers, your customers might find it interesting to know that your competition learns from you and that you're highly respected within your profession.

The wit and wisdom you share with these groups can mean literally thousands of dollars in your pocket from the new customers or clients generated from your speeches. Simply belonging to community organizations and selling hot dogs at the charity carnival will give you only a foot in the door. Those are dues all of us must pay for the right to be a part of a community. The bonus that you can bring to the table is to become "the expert" in your area on whatever you do. This starts with building your image.

You probably will discover that public speaking is the single quickest and least expensive way for you to build your image in your community or your industry. But public speaking can be a double-edged sword. You must do it right—a bad speech can cause irreparable damage. If you present information that your audience finds useless or simply bore them with a monotonal, uninspired presentation style, your career could suffer. That is the downside to using the public forum to promote yourself, and one of the goals of this book is to keep you and your audience from ever having to experience that.

A REALTOR®, for example, can use the recognition and trust gained from a professionally prepared presentation to pick up additional listing clients. Building trust is one of the single most critical reasons why people select the people with whom they wish to do business. In *How to Get Clients* (Warner Books), Jeff Slutsky writes that if you present your speech properly, your potential clients consider you the expert in your field, gaining a tremendous amount of credibility and exposure for yourself and your message.

Anyone Can Use Public Speaking as a Marketing Tool

Public speaking is effective in promoting just about any business or career. Frank Foster, an attorney specializing in copyrights, trademarks and patents, shared his expertise with the Ohio Chapter of the National Speakers Association (NSA), a group of about 100 professional speakers who write and produce original material. One of their biggest concerns is how to protect that information. Mr. Foster's seminar at this group's meeting was an excellent way to attract many potential clients who might need legal work done in this area.

Another member of NSA used the public speaking forum to inform women receiving chemotherapy about the wigs that she markets. She offered a free seminar, sponsored by the hospital, that the hospital marketed to prospective attendees as a public service. She found that she would usually sell about ten of these very high-quality wigs as a result. That would translate into about $10,000 in sales for a one-hour seminar. She had no marketing costs, and her only direct expenses were for the wigs. The rest was profit.

Duffy Spenser, Ph.D., is a social psychologist in Long Island. To help build her practice, she approached Nassau Community College about teaching a course for their adult education program.

Five hundred thousand catalogs are mailed each term to promote the course she offers. The adult ed program pays very little for teaching the course, but the exposure of half a million advertising pieces is worth it. Also, the credibility she gains through her association with the college further helps her promote her private practice.

*T*oasting a *M*aster
ZIG ZIGLAR

*Z*ig Ziglar, perhaps one of the most recognized names in professional public speaking, once told a National Speakers Association's audience that he spoke for free over 1,000 times before he ever gave his first paid presentation. As a matter of fact, Zig sold Michael Aun's mom and dad their first set of pots and pans when Zig was a student at the University of South Carolina in Columbia, South Carolina. In the kitchen table settings of several decades past, Zig developed the wit and charm he now displays before the thousands of people he addresses each year. Today, Zig commands huge speaking fees for some of the same stories he told across the kitchen table 30 years earlier. But the marketplace is now willing to pay those handsome fees because of the value his presentations provide. That tremendous value was begun and nurtured many years ago with those 1,000 plus free talks. That is where you hone your skills to become a proficient, and possibly even a professional, orator. Like Zig, most professional speakers learn their craft by giving many free speeches before they're able to get a fee.

Both Jeff Slutsky and Michael Aun make their living by giving speeches and seminars. They receive a fee for them and can't afford to do them free. Yet an opportunity arose that Jeff couldn't pass up–to be a presenter at the American Booksellers Association's (ABA) annual trade show, a massive event in which most publishers participate. His audience would be primarily bookstore owners and managers. When you're also selling books for a living, it is very exciting to have an opportunity to present your program to hundreds of people who can make your book successful.

Jeff is a big believer in free speech, but not necessarily free speeches. The ABA does not pay their speakers or reimburse their expenses! Normally, Jeff couldn't tie up a speaking date without an honorarium, but this event was an exception. Because the opportunity to advance his career was great, he agreed to speak, and one of his publishers paid his expenses.

As a result of this free speech, Jeff's publishers were pleased with the positive response and favorable publicity generated by the speech, and Jeff received great exposure in *Publishers Weekly*. And, of course, hundreds of booksellers heard and met him. This is a great benefit because, after all, they have hundreds of business book titles that they can offer their customers. Presenting at the ABA convention was so successful for all the parties that Jeff has presented his program at four different ABA conventions.

Starting in public speaking can be a challenge. For the novice looking for an audience, local clubs will not let you take their time unless you have something to say and know the right way to say it. That is why a forum like your local Toastmasters International club is a great place to start. You are given the opportunity to practice and improve.

What You Say and How You Say It

Public speaking consists of two main ingredients. The first is *style,* which involves your platform skills, including pacing, pitch, volume, use of humor, gestures, and so on. The second is your *message,* which involves your topic and content. Also, to a lesser degree, you have to consider the environment in which the presentation is made and your audience makeup, too.

You may be very accomplished at the techniques of public speaking, but until you take ownership of your message, you are just delivering a book report. Your topic and how you approach it is just as important as how you say it. Far too many speakers, professional and amateur, do not "walk their talk," or in other words, they often don't practice what they preach. They're teaching others how to do something that they themselves have not yet mastered.

You simply cannot afford to wing it. We live in a fast-paced, high-tech society that is visually oriented and sound-bite interested. People want information delivered with CNN timing and MTV pizzazz. Unfortunately, most new speakers don't take the time to ask and answer the basic question every audience member is asking, "What's in it for me?"

Speakers and communicators above all else must remember that they are in the information business. When they run out of ideas, they cease to be of value to the audience. So you have to inventory your "idea shelf." In short, you have to take ownership of the information you are imparting to others. How would you like to be operated on by a surgeon who had not been to school in ten years? The last thing you want to hear from this person is "oops."

Your audiences don't want to hear "oops," either. Regardless of whether you receive a fee or speak for free, the audience is paying you with their most valuable asset—their time. After all, they took the time to listen to what you had to say. That time is priceless and irreplaceable, and as long as you keep this in mind when preparing for a presentation, you dramatically increase your chance that your audience will walk away feeling that their time with you was well worth that investment.

Three Considerations When Preparing Your Speech

You should consider three key ideas when preparing your speech:

1. *Select a topic based on your goals.* Know the subject you want to present, based on an understanding of what your target audience wants or needs to hear. The subject or theme you choose must be appropriate to the audience and, at the same time, to your objectives. If your topic is "Advertising on a Shoestring Budget" and you wish to generate leads for future clients, an audience of junior high school students may be inappropriate. You might want to consider finding an audience of small business people or changing your topic to one more appropriate to teenagers, such as "the dangers of teens and drinking."

2. *Organize your content for best results.* Once you choose the appropriate topic (or audience), you need to share valuable substance or useful information about that sub-

ject. This may be a combination of statistical and anecdotal information to support your point of view.

In addition to the information you wish to share, you also have to consider how that information will be organized to best help your audience understand your key points. In a half hour after-lunch talk, you may have to choose between presenting one idea in great detail or presenting an overview of many ideas.

3. *Develop your unique style.* Your style is your unique method or technique for delivering the message to make the greatest impact on your audience. For example, think of how three popular singers would each sing *Row Row Row Your Boat:* Frank Sinatra, Madonna and Luciano Pavarotti. Even though it's the same sheet music and the same lyrics, you're going to get three vastly different interpretations of the same song. Each singer has his or her own unique style that gives that presentation its flavor or personality. Likewise, you'll begin to develop your unique style.

Preparation Is Paramount to Powerful Presentations

Even the most accomplished and experienced speaker would find it difficult to just stand up and have an audience instantly spellbound. Extemporaneous material is seldom extemporaneous. Most ad-libs are thought out well in advance. The bottom line of most successful presentations is simply doing your homework. Audiences want to know that you understand their special needs and interests. Even if your presentation is 95 percent "off the shelf," it's that extra 5 percent of tailoring that makes all the difference in the world. Keep in mind that the "off-the-shelf" portion may have taken many years to fine-tune.

For example, to prepare for a typical speech or seminar, Jeff Slutsky will ask the client for a list of six to eight people who would be considered some of the best marketing or salespeople in their group. He'll then interview them over the phone. He'll also review all the client's literature, including annual reports, brochures, manuals, newsletters, trade journals, and so on. Next, he'll call the client back and ask more questions based on the information he gathered to see which of his ideas and stories would be most appropriate and beneficial to their attendees. That work may account for only five minutes of a one-hour presentation, but it's a critical five minutes.

*T*oasting a *M*aster
JOEL WELDON

*J*oel Weldon is the master at preparation. When he speaks, he presents details about his clients and their companies that give the impression that he is one of them. Joel is famous for his intensive customization of presentations. Though he may be giving the same speech to two different audiences, the audiences feel that Joel developed the entire speech just for them. This is the mark of a real master.

Throughout speaking circles, including both Toastmasters International and the NSA, Joel is famous for his presentation entitled "Elephants Don't Bite." He delivered this speech to both organizations, geared for those different audiences, at their annual conventions. It remains one of the most heavily quoted presentations on the art of speaking that any speaker has ever delivered. Joel's philosophy is simple: Find out what the audience wants to hear and deliver it. Put them first, and in doing so, you will be able to better sell your message.

For example, when addressing a group of credit union executives, you always talk in terms of their "members," not "customers." Using the term "customers" screams out that you didn't do your homework. When addressing a group of Goodyear Tire dealers, Jeff memorized his tire size. So when he says in his speech, "Let's say a customer comes in and wants to get a price on a set of P225/50 ZR16 Eagle GSDs . . . ," right away he gains credibility with that audience. He did his homework.

☞ **Master's Tip:** *If you are going to use your communication skills to convey your message, make sure you have a message to communicate. Don't leave a* mess, *leave a* message.

Chapter 2

Developing and Compiling Your Material

*P*ossibly the single biggest downfall of many potential successful speakers is they fail to bring uniqueness to the platform. One reason is that they don't "walk their talk." Unfortunately, many of these speakers merely give "book reports," which means they present the information of other experts without contributing the added value of their own unique angle or twist.

Because of this lack of experience to share with their audiences, they destroy their credibility. Overcoming this failing of many speakers can be the edge you need to create a name for yourself as a speaker in your community.

Before you start developing your material, you must have a clear idea of the purpose of your speech. To help you understand this purpose, you may want to consider going through a few exercises. One approach would be to use a five-step exercise that progressively prepares you for gathering appropriate material. This exercise helps you develop both the content and the entertainment elements for your speech. Your first step is to choose your topic. The second step is to develop the benefit statement for your topic. Your third step is to then expand that benefit statement into a positioning statement. The fourth step is to use your positioning statement to develop your unique title. With these preliminary steps completed, your fifth step is to develop the "meat" of your program.

Choosing Your Topic

A *topic* is a relatively broad category that the content of your speech would fall under. To help you narrow down your topic, or subject, consider the categories that many speaker's groups use to categorize speakers:

advertising/public relations
alcoholism/drug abuse
arts/culture/music
athletics/sports
business
careers
change
character portrayals
communication
computers
consulting
creativity
customer service
diversity
education
empowerment
family
financial & tax planning
future
gender issues
government & politics
health & nutrition
human resources/labor relations
humor
image/self-esteem
inspirational
international affairs
law
leadership
magic
management

marketing/merchandising
media
medical/dental
motivation
negotiation
networking
organizational skills
patriotic
performance improvement
presentation skills
productivity
psychology
real estate
relationships
religion
retirement
sales
science/engineering
service provider
spouse programs
strategic planning
stress
success
team building
technology
time management/
    self-management
Total Quality Management
training
women in society
writing

The difficulty is to choose which category you feel best suits you. The NSA allows members to choose up to three different topics. For example, Jeff Slutsky's categories are advertising, marketing and sales. He could just as easily have chosen business, too. Michael Aun's topics are motivation, leadership and customer service. He is also well qualified to include retirement, financial planning and business.

The value in determining your topics is that they help a meeting planner decide whether you would be an appropriate speaker for their program. Of course, the downside is that you may not be considered for a certain presentation for which you were expertly qualified.

Here are some questions you can ask yourself when trying to select the perfect topic for you:

- What is of interest to me?
- What do I do for a living that would give me credibility on the platform?
- If I were a meeting planner, would I invite someone like me to give a speech to my group? Why?
- What compelled me to choose the career(s) I have chosen over the years?
- Why do I think my ideas would be of interest to others?
- Where else can I learn more about the particular topic on which I wish to speak?
- Who are the experts on this particular topic? What can I learn first from them?
- What intrigues me about a particular topic?
- How can I develop this enthusiasm into something special that my audiences will like?
- How can I be different from everyone else who has spoken on this particular topic?

Developing Your Title

Use the above topics as a guide for the next step, which is to develop a benefit statement and working title for your speech. This step takes those broad categories and helps you to more narrowly define your unique value on that particular topic by developing a title similar to the headline in an advertisement. It should give the potential user or buyer of your speech a benefit of listening and following your speech.

Writing the benefit statement.   In one or two sentences, write down what the benefit is. For example, one speaker in the area of financial planning specialized in working with well-to-do people to help them with accumulating wealth for retirement. The benefit statement that he developed was this: "I specialize in helping people accumulate over $1 million for their retirement while making modest monthly contributions." In his case, he had a specific amount of money they can shoot for while doing it without a lot of pain.

This benefit statement also is used often in advertising and even in meeting people. It's particularly useful when calling a meeting planner to get yourself booked as a speaker. Notice that there was no mention of financial planning in the benefit statement. That's the topic and therefore redundant.

Adding the positioning statement.   The next step is to build on your benefit statement by adding a second part that turns the benefit statement into a *positioning statement.* The part you add might describe your target audience or some unique problems or opportunities that you wouldn't address in your benefit statement. In addition to providing you with a stepping stone to developing your title, the benefit statement can also help you market your speech and perhaps even your business. The positioning statement, however, contains elements that you wouldn't use in your marketing or selling. It's for internal use only.

A positioning statement in our example might read like this: We specialize in *providing financial planning using primary insurance products for* helping people *55 years and older with an existing net worth of over $500,000 on how to* accumulate over $1 million for retirement while making modest monthly contributions. (The italicized parts are the additions to the benefit statement to make it a positioning statement.)

Creating your speech title.   Now with this preparatory exercise, you're ready to come up with a *working title.* It's called a working title because it is likely to change over time. Don't get so stressed about coming up with a perfect title. Some of the best titles evolved over time, so consider your title a work in progress.

You can use some creativity and "sizzle" in the title as long as it doesn't distract from the "selling" message of your title. Remember, when a meeting planner promotes the title of your speech to the membership, it has to be compelling enough to get the member to glance at the brief description of your presentation and decide if it is an event that they want to attend.

In the above example, one title might be, "Seven Easy Steps To Hatching a Million Dollar Nest Egg." To start you on this creative process, take two or three key words that you think should be in your title. In this case, some key words might be: *retirement, pension,* and *$1 million.* Then go to your thesaurus, jot down every variation of those key words, take all the variations of all of the key words, and start looking at every combination and permutation. This should get you thinking in the right direction. After that, it's trial, error and fine-tuning until you get what you discover works the best.

After completing this exercise, you're ready to collect and build material for your speech.

How You Can Walk Your Talk

Your own personal experiences are the best source of material for any presentation, whether it is a speech to the local Rotary Club on the upcoming Valentine's Ball or a keynote address before 25,000 people at a Positive Thinking Rally. To paraphrase the old expression, "you dance with the one who brought you," which is so appropriate. Every successful speech starts with a seed of interest, a basic idea on which the speaker wants to expound. You would no more plant a seed in barren ground than you should construct a speech on a weak foundation. Below are a number of ideas to help you get started.

No Penalty for Clipping

Immediately begin collecting ideas about the presentation that you want to make. Become a clipper. Collect articles on various topics that are related to the subjects about which you wish to speak. This means you need to subscribe to magazines and journals that pertain to your areas of interest. Keep a pair of scissors handy when reading these publications, and begin to cut out those articles that can provide additional substance to your topic. Be sure to jot down the publication, issue, date, and page number from where you clipped the article so you can substantiate your reference later in your speech or in your handout material.

Use a clipping service.   Another way to gather background information is by using a clipping service. This can be expensive, but you will get those articles you want to see from that month's current publications. Public relations firms generally use this type of service to find all articles written about their clients. You can give the service your criteria, as narrow or as broad as you wish, and their "readers" search thousands of dailies, weeklies and monthly publications looking for your "key words." They charge a monthly service fee (around $100/month) plus a set price per clipping.

Conduct Internet searches.   You might be able to get a fair amount of information by doing your own search over the Internet on your home computer. Many of the services have the current issues of major publications online, and you can pull from those sources to uncover material about your topics. The big advantage of doing an online search is that the cost is minimal, but it won't give you the breadth of a search you get from a clipping service. The other element you have to consider is that *you* have to do the work, whereas a clipping service simply sends the clips to you on a regular basis.

Do library computer searches.   Your local library can provide you with a wealth of information on your topics, including a computerized bibliography of every book written on your subject. It's a good idea to be aware of all those books, regardless of publication date, because you need to know what other perceived experts are saying, whether you agree with them or not.

The other service available at your local library is a *periodical search.* Similar to a search you can do on your computer at home, your library's computer searches over a much greater stable of publications and over many years. So by putting your key words into the search, you can get a listing of articles written about your topic, most of which contain a brief summary. Sometimes you can lift a great quote from the summary, but if an article appears to be of great value to your research, you then have the ability to retrieve that entire article.

Tips on successful media searches.   When conducting searches, either on your own or through a clipping service, you need to come up with the key words that will trigger the clipper or computer to provide you with those articles or summaries related to your topic. For example, if you speak on customer service for small business, you would use two different key word strings: "customer service" and "small business." The more specific you are, the fewer clippings you get, but those that you do get are probably geared more toward your topic. Using a similar search with the key words, "service" and "business," for example, will provide you with a greater number of responses, but much of them may not be useful to you.

Through trial and error you can begin to narrow down the ideal word strings you need to use to get the best results. If you want to limit your search to customer service stories that specifically deal with restaurants, quick-oil-change places, and video rental stores, you would probably want to conduct at least three different searches. If several words are interchangeable with one of your word strings, you might want to run separate searches using these variations. If your computer software is more sophisticated, it might allow for "and/or" options in the search. In the example above, you could plug in: "customer service" and "restaurants" or "eating places" or "dining out." This format will search for stories that involve customer service for any of the other three.

Use interns.   To help you with your searches, you might employ the services of a college intern. If your local university or college has a journalism or speech department, you could contact a professor and offer an internship program where the student(s) can get some practical experience. However, don't feel limited to journalism or speech departments; you might find a professor in another department who would appreciate being able to provide this kind of experience to his or her students. You have to find a hook. If your topic is business-related, you could also contact the business department. The same might apply for economics, sociology, and so on. If you can find a way to tie your topic or use of your speech to a department within a college, junior college or university, this link will give you an advantage when approaching the professors.

You may want to pay minimum wage and see if you can arrange with the professor to provide credit for the internship. This may mean a little extra paperwork for you, but you'll attract some highly motivated candidates with the lure of both credit and something they can put on a resume.

Interview research.   Up to this point, you've been gathering information that already exists. However, to make your content unique, you might want to consider creating your own information. One way to do this is to interview people who are experts on your topic or portions of your topic whose expertise you wish to share in your speech. For example, if your topic is on "the most common mistakes made in sport fishing," you may want to interview someone from your local Department of Natural Resources. You may be able to interview, either by phone or in person, the president of a local club or association on fishing, talk to the managers or owners of sporting goods stores or bait and tackle shops. With any luck, you'll have a unique anecdote, observation, or valuable statistic or two from one of these sources that you can then use to "spice" up the meat of your program.

Survey research.   Another form of proprietary research would be a survey designed to gather statistics about an aspect of your topic. Professional surveys are very costly, but you can conduct your own relatively cheaply. You can use three survey methods. The first is the telephone survey. Call a list of prospects and ask them a handful of questions (usually no more than five or six) about their opinions on a given subject. It helps to give your respondents multiple choice answers from which to choose. Be sure to design your questions so that the answers you receive are not biased.

If you're conducting a lighter program that is geared more for entertainment, you might consider doing a mini-survey to help reinforce a point. In this respect, you are using statistics like a drunk uses a lamp post, more support than illumination. Jeff Slutsky used this approach when he was developing his speech based on his book, *How to Get Clients.* His premise was that professionals in law firms and accounting firms value employees who can bring in new business more than those who could crank out the work. To confirm his theory, he called a half dozen partners of different law firms and accounting firms and asked them the following question: "If you had two young lawyers (or accountants) working for you and one was a 2.0 GPA partier who graduated from Ohio State but could bring in several hundred thousands dollars of new billable hours of business a year, and the other a 4.0 Harvard grad with honors who did good work but brought in no clients, who would make partner first?" In every instance the partier from Ohio State was selected.

While not statistically significant, this informal survey provides anecdotal evidence that the topic was on target.

Other methods for getting some statistics is to do a direct mail survey. If your topic is geared for a general audience, you might be able to conduct a customer intercept survey at a high traffic area like a grocery store or department store exit. Of course, you'll want to get permission to do this. And don't forget to use your interns as a great way to handle a lot of this work.

One other place you may want to look for unique information is at a research company that conducts "generic" surveys on many different topics that you can buy or subscribe to. This can be very costly, but usually it is more reasonable than having custom research done. And, of course, this assumes that the surveys they conduct apply to your needs.

The group you're speaking to also may have their own research that you can borrow to "tailor" your presentation to their needs. Ask the association or corporation meeting planner to provide you with information that you can incorporate into your presentation. Jeff Slutsky did this prior to presenting his marketing seminar for the National Marine Manufacturers Association (NMMA). The audience consisted of 300 retail boat dealers. The NMMA had conducted a very extensive survey about the buying habits of boat owners. One interesting statistic from their survey was that 8 percent of existing boat owners said that they were in the market for a new boat in the next 12 months. By a quick show of hands in the seminar, Jeff determined that the average dealer had about 300 active customers in the database. That meant that 80 potential new boat sales were on that average list. The key was to find out who were the 80 ready to buy and then give them a reason for stopping in. That seminar taught the dealers the techniques for unlocking and using this key piece of information.

In this presentation, the audience was very motivated to listen because they had some hard numbers to justify the value of the approach.

Keep other sources in mind. Michael Aun also collects audiotapes and videotapes and has categorized these in a fashion similar to organizing clipped and other material. His tape library is broken down by the source of the tapes. For instance, he gets a monthly audiocassette tape from the NSA called *Voice of Experience.* He keeps all those tapes in a section labeled NSA.

Michael also receives monthly tapes from other sources as well. For instance, the General Agents and Managers Association, of which he's a member, gives him an album in which to insert each of their monthly tapes. If the source does not provide an album, he simply purchases a tape box and sets it aside for that source.

If you want to speak on business-related topics, you could subscribe to condensation services like Soundview Executive Summaries. This service summarizes and boils many of the current leading business books down to eight pages. This gives you an understanding of the main concepts, and you may discover a good piece of information to quote. It also lets you know if it is a book you should buy and study. There are audio services too that summarize, on cassette tape, leading business books and news magazines.

The great speaker, Joel Weldon, CPAE,* of Scottsdale, Arizona, once remarked, "Find out what everybody else is doing, then don't do it!" That is as solid a piece of advice that anyone can give any would-be speaker. The purpose of your research should be to confirm what you already know about the topic or disprove your hypothesis. Research is not about stealing another's ideas and making them your own.

---

*CPAE (Council of Peers Award for Excellence) is an award for platform excellence from the National Speakers Association (NSA). Selections are based on nominations made by the current CPAEs, and awards are limited to a maximum of five each year. A committee of seven members judge each candidate on the originality of their material, uniqueness of style, experience, delivery technique, image, reputation, professionalism, and ability to relate to their audiences.

Craft Your Own Unique Stories

The best way to enhance information and make it your own is to create examples and anecdotes based on your personal experiences. These stories can be humorous or dramatic, and usually give your audience a little bit of self-disclosure. Audiences connect with a speaker who is willing to share a little of him or herself with them. They don't necessarily need to know all the details of a certain event, but you can use those relevant experiences to help your audience better understand your point while building that rapport.

Developing your own illustration, through anecdotes and case histories, is the most challenging element in creating material for a speech. Many less experienced speakers tend to use stories they've heard in other speaker's programs. There is a place for this, provided you have obtained permission from that speaker to use that material. But, by far, the best material is original.

Once you have worked out the main content of your speech, think back to any experiences you personally have had that may reinforce a point in that speech. In a speech on customer service, you would probably recall several great examples of both good and bad customer service. In a motivational speech where you want your audience to overcome some obstacle, it helps them if you yourself had experienced that problem, then share with them exactly how you overcame or solved it.

As you continue to use a certain story in a speech, you'll begin to fine-tune it with experience. The more you tell the story, the more you'll begin to see your audience's reactions to certain parts. You'll start to embellish the story and expand on it. Perhaps you'll introduce new elements to the story from other events you've experienced or have been told to you by audience members. The more observant you are about even what may seem to be an insignificant occurrence, the more you'll have to work with when flushing out your speech.

A great way to help better understand this is by attending your local Toastmasters International club meetings. Watch some of the more experienced members in your group. This is not to steal their material or emulate their style but rather to get a feel for how people do it.

Another way to get a feel for how speakers develop their unique material is to attend some meetings of your NSA chapter. Usually at these meetings, you'll have an opportunity to see several professional speakers. Many of these chapters have an annual "showcase," which is a great place to view many speakers in a single day. Showcases are events where up to 20 speakers get a brief period of time to share their best stuff. The audience is primarily meeting planners who might be in the market to hire these speakers. However, attendance is generally open, and for a reasonable fee you can see many different topics and speaking styles.

Remember, your goal is to develop your own unique style, not copy someone else's.

Putting Some Meat in Your Program

Most of the information-gathering tactics suggested are great for obtaining some statistical, and, perhaps to a lesser degree, some anecdotal evidence to support your points. To drive home those points, though, you need to develop compelling, entertaining or humorous stories.

For example, Jeff Slutsky is perhaps the leading expert in and speaker on the topic of local-level advertising, marketing, and promotion using a shoestring budget. The topic itself has a benefit to a great many business people, yet there's no sizzle. So he calls his particular approach to this topic *Street Fighter Marketing & Sales,* and it immediately gets people's attention. "Street fighter" is the sizzle, while *local level advertising, marketing and promotion using a shoestring budget* is the steak.

In this seminar, he combines some hard-hitting "how-to's" with interesting and funny examples to illustrate this "street fighter's" attitude. For example, when Jeff is explaining about how street fighters deal with competitors that use low-ball prices, he explains to his attendees that price is an issue, but not the only issue, in making the buying decision.

Then he tells them about a hair salon owner who worked very hard at developing a good clientele. The owner provided super service and quality work. He would charge $15 for a haircut, which put him in the mid-range for that marketplace. Well, a new shopping center was built directly across the street from this guy. And in that shopping center was one of those discount haircut franchises. To advertise this new franchise, the owner rented a billboard right in front of the shopping center. It had a plain blue background and plain letters that read, "We Give $6 Haircuts." Well, all these people going to their $15 haircut appointments over the course of the month saw this big billboard across the street that says, "We Give $6 Haircuts," and many of them gave the competitor a try.

What's this salon owner going to do? He can't compete on price. He could cut his price in half and still not compete. But he's a street fighter. So he buys the billboard in front of his own salon, uses the same blue background and the same plain white letters, and puts, "WE FIX $6 HAIRCUTS!" Turned them around instantly. Price is an issue, but it's not the only issue.

Later in that seminar, Jeff talks about all the promotional opportunities a business has within three to five miles of their location, and he shows a map of a typical community on the screen. He continues,

> This is a map of your typical neighborhood. This one happens to be my neighborhood, a suburb of Columbus, Ohio, called Gahanna, Ohio. "Gahanna" happens to be the Hebrew word for "hell." And "Ohio" is the Japanese word for "Good Morning." So Gahanna is actually "Good Morning, Hell" in two languages.

How did Jeff come up with these lines? While at a speakers convention, Jeff was talking with his good friend and fellow speaker and author, Dr. Carl Hammerschlag. During the conversation, Jeff mentioned to Carl that he and his brother Marc had just bought an office building in Gahanna, which is a suburb of Columbus. Carl speaks fluent Hebrew and German and casually mentioned to Jeff that "Gahenna" (correct spelling) is the Hebrew word for hell. Jeff thought that was funny. So he mentioned it in his next seminar on neighborhood marketing, and sure enough, it got some laughs.

Jeff also had taken Japanese for his foreign language requirement in college and knew that "ohayo," pronounced just like the state, was the Japanese word for "Good Morning." That led him to add the line about "Good Morning, Hell, in two languages," which also got some laughs.

From several unconnected experiences, one recent and one over ten years earlier, Jeff was able to interject a little humor in his seminar that helped his audience better understand his key points.

Not only that, most of his audiences also remember where he lives, which is a great marketing move in its own right when you're looking to develop additional spinoff business from your seminars.

While showing the map of Gahanna on the overhead projector or using a participant's workbook, Jeff goes on to point out all the potential promotional opportunities like the typical fast-food places, video rental stores, discount stores, schools, churches, major employers, a hospital, etc.

☞ Master's Tips:

1. *Become a clipper.*
2. *Learn to scan, not just read material.*
3. *Invest in a library card.*
4. *Subscribe to publications that specialize in your topic.*
5. *Read books on your topic: keep a highlighter handy.*
6. *Listen to audiocassettes, and view videos of other speakers on your topic.*
7. *Subscribe to newspapers and publications on your topic.*
8. *Design a collection system, for example, a journal, a computer, a file system, a three-ring binder program, a clipping service, an on-line service, and so forth.*
9. *Commit an hour per day to finding material on your topic, and become as familiar as possible with the data.*
10. *Subscribe to book and news summary services.*

Chapter 3

*U*sing Humor to Make Your Point

*H*umor can be a critical part of an effective presentation when you use it properly. When you can get an audience to laugh with you, it not only helps to keep your audience interested in your speech but also helps break down some of the resistance they may have had toward your ideas. In addition, when you reinforce a key point with appropriate humor, your audience is more likely to remember it. According to Melvin Helitzer, author of *Comedy Writing Secrets: How to Think Funny, Write Funny, Act Funny, and Get Paid for It* (Writer's Digest Books), "Humor is a universal speech opener because it immediately gets us respectful attention. It's psychologically impossible to hate someone with whom you've laughed."

Is humor critical to a successful speech? "You don't have to use humor in a speech unless you want to get paid," says Bill Gove, CSP,* CPAE, long regarded as one of America's premier keynote speakers and humorists. But if you're not looking to become a fee-

---

*CSP (Certified Speaking Professional) is the highest earned designation presented by the National Speakers Association (NSA). It recognizes a commitment to ongoing education, proven speaking experience, and ethical behavior. It is awarded to individuals who have completed a comprehensive application process and met the criteria set by NSA.

paid, professional speaker, it may not be critical to you. Some of the most memorable speeches in history have no humor. Lincoln didn't have one funny line in the Gettysburg Address. John F. Kennedy didn't once mention his mother-in-law when he said, "Ask not what your country can do for you." Martin Luther King didn't open up with a joke when he mesmerized his audience with, "I had a dream." Certain situations simply don't lend themselves to humor.

Guidelines for Using Humor

But if humor is appropriate for your speech and you use appropriate humor in your speech, you can make unimagined impact with your audience. The downside of humor is that it is very difficult to get it right. Here are some guidelines when considering using humor in your presentation:

1. *Humor should be used only by people who are funny.* Some people just aren't funny. If that is the case with you, perhaps you should consider not using humor in your speech. There is nothing worse than a speaker trying to be funny, who is obviously not. It's embarrassing to the speaker and to the audience.

2. *Humor should be original.* The best humor is original. It doesn't have to be a joke. It could be an amusing anecdote about a personal experience you had. Using somebody else's humor is dangerous. First, you should always get their permission to quote them, and second, you should always state your source. Once you develop original humor, it is yours forever. It's unique, and there's no danger of following another speaker who uses the same joke, line, pun or story as you. This repetition is very embarrassing. Sometimes it's possible to adapt an old joke or story with a new twist that is relevant to your message.

3. *Humor should be funny.* What you think is funny may not be funny to your audience. You need to try it out on people to watch their reactions. Developing humor is not so much science as art. It's more like the way Thomas Edison developed the light bulb—a lot of trial and error. If a line or story

just doesn't get the reaction you want, give serious thought to taking it out of your presentation.

4. *Humor should be appropriate.* Different types of audiences react to different types of humor. Consider your audience makeup when choosing which funny stories or lines you're going to use. A funny story that gets a super reaction from an audience of New York teenagers might not work for a group of senior citizens in St. Petersburg. Tailor your humor for your audience.

5. *Humor should be relevant.* Humorous examples work best when illustrating a key point in your presentation. You're not there to be a stand-up comic. You're there to sell your ideas to your audience, so make sure that when you use humor it helps you do just that. The more relevant the humor, the less funny it has to be to make impact.

6. *Humor should be laudatory.* As a rule, never embarrass or insult an audience member or a segment of your audience with your humor. When using an audience member as the object of humor, it must be done with a high degree of sensitivity and generally with prior permission from your subject.

7. *Humor can be self-deprecating.* Self-deprecating humor can be very effective and can help develop a special rapport with audience members. For example, Michael Aun pokes fun at himself and the fact that he's overweight. According to Michael, "I have been heavy since I graduated from high school. A friend of mine once told me, 'Use it or lose it.' Since I have never been successful in losing weight, I use it in my presentations. Some of the lines are old and worn—'I get my shoes shined, I have to take the guy's word for it.'"

Other lines have been created by other circumstances. For instance, since 1974, Michael has been in the life insurance business. He's well insured. In fact, he's his own best client. Michael often quips to his audiences about his wife giving him a hard time about his weight, "I tell her, 'Don't sweat it. We don't have any problems that death won't clear up. I'm well insured.'"

Jeff is 5'4". He often hears, "You look much taller in your video." He replies, "You want to know why I'm so short?

It's because everybody keeps asking me for an idea off the top of my head. I used to be 6'1"."

8. *Humor should be clean.* Even if someone is laughing on the outside at a line or story that is off color, they may be crying on the inside. Every time you use profanity, you are at risk of alienating an audience member. Some speakers feel a well placed "hell" or "damn" is necessary for them to get their point across or for the humor to shine through. Others would argue this with them. Some audiences react negatively to certain kinds of innuendo and double entendre, while others just love it. Be careful and know your audience. No ethnic jokes unless they're self-deprecating. No religious jokes unless they're self-deprecating. No handicap jokes unless they're self-deprecating. Several years ago there was a line going around a speakers convention, "Have you heard about the new organization, DAM? Mothers Against Dyslexia." Though it takes a moment to sink in, it gets a laugh and probably would be acceptable. Be very careful with political jokes unless you're a politician. Be careful with jokes about being overweight or bald, especially if you aren't. Someone is bound to be offended. A good rule of thumb is "When in doubt, leave it out!"

9. *Humor should be told with skill and timing.* The words of a funny line are simply not enough. The presentation of that line is just as critical to making the line work. A really good presenter can take a mediocre line or story and get the most out of it. Johnny Carson, the former host of *The Tonight Show,* was a master at this. Sometimes the bad jokes got the most laughs because of the style in which he presented. Comedian Rich Little, telling the same joke while doing an impression of Johnny Carson, might be funnier yet. Same joke. Different presentation style.

Developing Your Humor

Be Observant

A funny story or anecdote is often developed by simply being observant. Personal experiences and observations are the best way to develop original humor for two reasons: First, no one could tell a personal experience about you like you can. You lived it. And second, since the story is about you, it is more difficult for some other speaker to "borrow" that material.

Creating good original humor is tough but very rewarding. In fact, a lot of time is devoted to this subject at breakout sessions during NSA conventions. Jeanne Robertson, CPAE, former president of NSA, is a genius at developing humor. Many of her techniques might be useful as you develop your own material. She will often take a funny line and work backward to create the story around the punch line.

For years, Jeanne has been keeping journals, collecting funny events that have happened to her on the way to airports, in taxis or at beauty contests. She is a former Miss North Carolina who came in 49th the year she competed for Miss America. "Thank God for the girl from Mississippi who played the comb," quips Jeanne. "It had several teeth missing."

Jeanne brags about being the tallest woman ever to have competed in a Miss America pageant. She adds, "I'm also the tallest woman ever to have lost a Miss America pageant."

Jeanne's whole presentation is built around her experiences in the Miss America pageant. Her now famous baton story is a classic. She tells about a young lady who threw a baton in the air at a local pageant but it didn't come down. Jeanne's stories are uniquely hers. If anyone else tried to tell those stories, they would not work unless they were 6'2" and had competed in a Miss America pageant.

As Jeanne tells these wonderful stories, she uses props, such as the baton. (See Chapter 4 on props for more detail.) They help to make the story real. Most of all, Jeanne has the clever ability to put the audience into the story, which is what humor is supposed to do.

Enhance Your Humorous Story

According to Carl Hurley, EdD, CSP, CPAE, from Lexington, Kentucky, and a nationally recognized humorist, "There are three ways to develop a funny story: Tell it the way it happened; Tell it the way it happened, sort of; Tell it the way it *could have* happened." Enhancement and embellishment of an actual event are the cornerstone for developing really funny material. Here's an account of an experience that Jeff Slutsky had when he nearly missed a very important speaking date. First, take a look at a transcript of this segment of his speech:

When you run a small business, you can't afford to mess up because even an honest mistake can do major damage to your company's reputation and bottom line unless you think and act fast. I had such an experience when I was confirmed six months in advance to deliver my "Confessions of a Street Fighter" keynote speech on a Monday morning for Sony Corporation in Marco Island, Florida. The top 150 retail dealers had to win a sales contest to attend a special convention there.

Well, six months goes by a lot faster than you can imagine. I stroll in the house at about two in the morning . . . I was out doing research . . . when I get an urgent phone call from my brother. In a panic, he tells me I was supposed to be in Marco Island for my 9:00 AM speech! He says that the client had been calling me at home and finally got a hold of him. I try to calm him down and tell him that it wasn't until the following Monday. He insists I look at my calendar, which I do. He is right! The blood rushes from my head, and a feeling of panic comes over me. It is my fault. How did this happen? It doesn't matter. The first thing I do is call my contact in his hotel room at Marco Island. He's practically in tears and fears for his job if I don't show. I tell him I'd call him back soon while I try to figure something out.

I know for a fact that there are not a lot of nonstop flights between Columbus, Ohio, and Marco Island, Florida, at 2:30 in the morning. I frantically start looking in the Yellow Pages for charter planes to see if there is any way I can get down there in the next six hours. I dial one after another after another. No one is answering at two in the morning. How can these people run a business like that? After the tenth try, someone answers. It is an air ambulance service. I say I have a medical emergency and need to be in Marco Island by 9:00 this morning. "What's the nature of your emergency, sir?" "If I'm not at Marco Island by 9:00 this morning, this guy is gonna kill me!" He responds by asking me a very important question, "Do you have an American Express Card?" I say, "Yes." He says, "No problem." It turns out they have these Lear Jet ambulances on 30 minutes standby at different cities throughout the country, with one in Detroit. It comes with a pilot, copilot and a registered nurse; it's a package deal. He then tells me that the flight from Columbus to Marco is just two hours and the Marco airport just five minutes from the hotel. They could pick me up in two hours and still get me there several hours before my speech.

I call the client back and tell him that I had chartered a Lear Jet and I would be there by 7:00 AM. I rush to my office to get my *Street Fighter Marketing* books and tapes, then I grab a two-liter bottle of diet soda out of the refrigerator and run off to the airport. With my adrenaline still surging while waiting for the jet to arrive, I start pacing back and forth replaying in my mind how I got myself in this mess. The whole time I'm drinking out of this two-liter bottle. In a little over 20 minutes, I polish off the entire two-liter bottle of diet soda . . . with caffeine. I don't need a jet now. It lands 10 minutes later. I get on board and we take off.

About 20 minutes into the flight, I realize I just drank a two-liter bottle of diet soda. Now, this jet has everything you can imagine, except one thing. They don't expect their customers to be able to get up and go. And since they know that I am not their standard medical emergency, they didn't bother to bring along the usual containers and bedpans. There was no way I could wait another 90 minutes, and it's not like at 41,000 feet you can just roll down the window. Another rush of panic is beginning to surface when the nurse tells me, "I have a solution to your problem." "Anything, what?" "Catheterization!" (pause)

I quickly realize that I have to give a very important speech in a few hours and don't need to do it in an unfamiliar octave. I then crawl up to the pilots and ask what they do on long trips. The pilot reaches into his leather map case and pulls out a sack lunch. Inside the sack lunch he has a bunch of carrot sticks in a Glad® baggie with a zip-top lock. He empties out the carrot sticks and hands the baggie to me. Then with the most serious face I've ever seen in my life, he says, "When you're done, make sure the strip at the top turns green!" It worked great. As a matter of fact, I don't travel anywhere without one. (At this point, Jeff reaches into his inside coat pocket, pulls one out and shows it to the audience.)

My plane lands a little before 7:00 AM. As I'm just stepping off, the pilot asks me how long I'm going to be. Well, the speech is going to be just under an hour, and with signing books and answering questions, I figure I will be done sometime before noon. "Great, we'll wait." The return trip is free. They have to go right by Columbus anyway. What a bargain. The limo gets me to the hotel in plenty of time to clean up and prepare. I then gave one of the best presentations of my life. Everything clicked perfectly. Pure adrenaline. When I finished, I stayed around a little to answer questions and sign books, then back to the airport.

The client was very impressed and appreciative that I was able to honor my commitment to them and was willing to do it regardless of the cost. Oh yes . . . the cost. It was $7,000. Then to pour just a little salt into the wound, they tack on a 10 percent excise tax because it was a passenger ticket. I thought on the way back that had I been catheterized I might argue that it was a medical expense and I could have saved $700! Actually, in retrospect, it was perhaps the best $700 I ever spent.

Now the reason I share this story with you is that the client was ecstatic and has called back several times since. Plus, because it was such an unusual story, I got a lot of word-of-mouth exposure with other potential clients. I can safely say that I got back my "investment" many times over, and the reason is that I never lost sight of my priorities. Keeping your promises to your client never costs . . . it always pays.

This is one of Jeff's most remembered stories, and it always gets a big response from his audiences. It also makes a very important point, "Always make good on your promises to your clients." It contains all the necessary elements to make a funny anecdote: The event itself was true, so his story is original. Jeff tells it with polish and timing. It's self-deprecating but insults nobody or any group. It has an important message that is relevant to his speech.

So did it actually happen the way Jeff says it does? Well, in the philosophy of Carl Hurley, "sort of." Everything is completely factual and accurate right up to the time he calls to order the ambulance jet. It did, in fact, cost him $7,700. At the last minute, the dispatcher was able to find a Lear jet with an "Executive Configuration." So it really wasn't an ambulance jet, and no registered nurse was on the flight. But in developing the story for maximum impact from the platform, he embellished it with "what originally was supposed to happen," which makes the story funnier.

Because of that embellishment, he was able to add the "catheterization" line, which gets a big laugh. This took some work to get it just right. He told it several different ways, but he realized that to get the maximum laugh from the line, he had to put the word "catheterization" at the very end of the sentence so as soon as he said it, he could pause. Originally, he would say, "The nurse wanted to catheterize me." It got a good laugh. But when he changed the line to, "'I have a solution to your problem.' 'Anything, what?' 'Catheterization!'" it got a maximum laugh. Then he used an actual ziplock baggie as a prop for another big laugh. The story just keeps building. (Note: If you would like to see a video of Jeff presenting this story along with four others, you can get his demo video for $10 plus $5 shipping and handling. Send your check, money order, Visa, MasterCard, or American Express order to Demo Video, Street Fighter Marketing, 467 Waterbury Court, Gahanna, OH 43230; 800-758-8759 [800-SLUTSKY].

Personal experiences are still the best way to develop original humor. Take an event that happened to you to reinforce the point you're trying to make. Jeff has also used a story about a sales technique called the "echo." In this segment of his speech, he is sharing with the audience the idea that it is important to ask lots of questions and listen to what the other person is saying if you want to successfully address the needs of your customers. For years, he shared an experience he had with a former girlfriend. His wife heard the story and insisted that he stop telling that story about his ex-girlfriend. This put Jeff in a quandary. The story worked great. It would always get a big laugh and helped drive home a key point. Instead, he altered it slightly so that the girlfriend later became his wife. That change didn't add a thing to the story, but it didn't take away anything either. But oddly enough, after making that requested change, it allowed Jeff to add four more funny lines that he couldn't have developed unless he had made that little alteration. Here's an excerpt from Jeff's story. The italicized text is the material that he added after the change:

> One way to stay in control of the conversation and at the same time gain a lot of valuable information is to use a technique called the "echo." I first learned this a number of years ago from Bill Bishop, a sales trainer in Orlando, and it really works great.

Here is how the echo technique works. You wait until your customer is done talking. If you want additional details about that particular subject, you simply echo the last word, two words, three words at the most, and repeat them back to the customer in the form of a question. So it might sound something like this (using the audience as an example):

"I'm going to fly to Las Vegas."

"Las Vegas?"

"Yeah, I'm doing a seminar for ABC Company."

"ABC Company?"

"Oh, yeah. They're a great bunch of guys."

"Bunch of guys?"

"Oh, you should see them when they start to party."

"Party?"

So in this way, you can keep somebody talking and get all this valuable information that can help you discover useful tips on doing business with them. When Bill first told me this technique, I was dying to try it out. I was flying back to Columbus, Ohio, from Orlando, Florida, and my girlfriend, *who later became my wife,* was going to pick me up at the airport. I thought this would be a perfect time to try it out. She always complained that I didn't pay too much attention to her, which was pretty much on target, so I thought this might just help turn things around. I got into the car. Instead of staring off into space as I usually did when I returned from a trip, I turned to her and led off with a question, "How was work today?"

She was excited. I was paying attention to her and her eyes lit up. "Work was really crazy today. They sent this guy in from the corporate office to do a quarterly report."

"Quarterly report?"

"Yeah. They send someone in every three months or so to make sure we're on target and going to hit our projections."

"Projections?"

"Oh, yeah. See, last year we were down quite a bit, and our quota is to increase the quarter at least 12 percent."

"Twelve percent?"

"At least! If we do it, the entire department gets a big bonus!"

"Big bonus?"

"They are going to send us on a trip!"

"Trip?"

I kept her going for 35 minutes all the way home from the airport. I did not say more than 25 words. I knew everything about her life and she very little about mine . . . which was pretty much what I wanted. She thought I was the most warm, sensitive, caring individual in the world. *One year later, I closed that sale! Then about eight-and-a-half months later we had a little spin-off business. (pause with guilty look on face) About three years after that, some repeat spin-off business . . . (pause) . . . and then buyer's remorse. (pause) I suppose the service after the sale was just a little weak.*

Looking for Humor in All the Right Places

Humor is everywhere. Your job is to notice it. Let's look at some examples of humor that can work effectively in presentation.

Using cartoons.   One of the most successful speakers in America finds his humor on the funny pages themselves. Philip D. Steffen, CSP, CPAE, of the Bottom Line Group in Marietta, Georgia, loves using cartoons on an overhead or slide projector. You, too, can often find a cartoon that helps to reinforce a point you're making in your presentation.

Phil and Michael Aun have shared hundreds of platforms together over the years, Phil is a consummate professional when it comes to using this kind of humor. He always credits the author of the material. He never uses the material just for the sake of using it but lets the material support important points that he wants to make in the presentation. You can read aloud the caption to your audience if it leads directly to the point you're making. Some speakers even put the cartoon on the screen for the audience to read for themselves.

Employing funny signs.   For years, Michael has been collecting funny signs that he refers to in the course of his presentation. Many of these signs came out of books on humor; others he has actually witnessed. Some came from members of his audience or his employees. One of Michael's most popular speeches has to do with "effective communication." He stresses that many people actually don't communicate what they really mean to say. To illustrate this point, he shares the messages that appear on some miscommunicated signs. Here are a few examples:

Sign in Warsaw Hotel
"The manager has personally passed all the water served here."

Sign in Portuguese Dry Cleaners
"Drop your trousers here for best results."

Sign in a Copenhagen Airline Ticket Office
"We take your bags and send them in all directions."

Sign in a Paris Dress Shop
"Because of the big rush,
we will execute customers in strict rotation."

Sign in a Zurich Hotel
"Because of the impropriety of entertaining guests
of the opposite sex in the bedroom,
it is suggested that the lobby be used for this purpose."

Sign in a Paris Elevator
"Please leave your values at the front desk."

Sign in an Athens Hotel
"Visitors are expected to complain at the office
between the hours of 9 and 11 AM daily."

Funny signs are everywhere, but you must be on the lookout for them and must have a system of collecting the data. You might want to carry a journal for jotting down these ideas. Don't trust your memory: write things down. As you write them down, try to also think of key points in your seminar where they might apply.

(For a free audiotape or videotape catalog of Michael using signs in his presentation, contact: Michael Aun, P.O. Drawer 701385, St. Cloud, FL 34770-1385; 407-870-0030 or 800-356-0567 or fax 407-870-2088; aunline@prodigy.)

Recycling Old Material for a New Twist

One way to develop original humor is to take an old story or joke and rework it using your own experiences. Jeff Slutsky does this with his opening example of the "street fighter's" attitude. He shares with his audience an experience he had with a client who ran an appliance store and needed a solution. His customers spent a lot of his time going over the features and benefits of a refrigerator, freezer or perhaps a TV set. After all that work, the customer would leave to go price shop with three or four competitors in the area. The client asked Jeff whether the client could do anything to keep these people from shopping around so much, or better yet, if they could just visit his place last, he would at least have a decent shot of selling them his appliances. What could he do?

Jeff had him do a number of different things, one of which was an idea he had heard about five years earlier that was used by a manufactured mobile home salesperson. Jeff adapted this idea to his client's situation and told him to fill one of his freezers with half gallons of ice cream. Then, when a customer was ready to leave without buying, the sales force was instructed to give that person, absolutely free, a half gallon of ice cream, just for stopping in. Well, naturally, the customer's hearts would melt with enthusiasm for the store. And when they got in their car to shop at a couple of other places, on a hot July day, holding this half gallon of ice cream, they realized they had a little problem on their hands. They had to immediately go home and put that half gallon of ice cream in the freezer. As a result, the store's sales went up that year by 13.5 percent according to an article in *The Wall Street Journal.*

This is an old idea that Jeff suggested to his client. What makes it work in Jeff's speech is that Jeff's client actually used the idea and Jeff then shares this personal experience with the audience. Jeff first started using this story in speeches in 1979, and while the original idea wasn't his, the anecdote is because it's based on his own experience.

Making a Strong Impression

You can make a story or a line much funnier if you have the ability to use dialects and impersonations. Hope Mihalap, CPAE, has a delightfully funny presentation about cultural diversity and uses different dialects and personal stories to get across her message. Steve Rizzo, East Islip, New York, is a comedian who has been featured on Showtime and HBO. He's adapted his humor for speeches on using humor to help deal with stress. Steve uses impressions to make his funny material even funnier. His speech centers around the concept of seeing the humor in life to help deal with everyday stresses. Somehow, a key point just sounds funnier when the presenter can do it in the voice of Jack Nicholson or Jerry Lewis. Make sure you try out your impressions or dialects on a practice audience first and be sure to make the routine relevant to your point. Also be sure that your use of impressions and dialects is in good taste and will not offend anyone in your audience.

Combining Music and Humor

If you have some real musical talent, you might consider combining it with humor to make a very memorable presentation. There are many terrific speakers who use humor and music together in a presentation, including Doc Blakely, CSP, CPAE, and Rosita Perez, CSP, CPAE. Doc and his son, Mike, of Wharton, Texas, do a father-son musical comedy routine that the audiences just love. They incorporate singing and dancing into their show and have liberal use of humorous lines and anecdotes.

Rosita Perez in Gainesville, Florida, is a former mental health counselor turned professional speaker who makes a powerful point in her speech about prejudice and reinforces that point using music and dialect. She begins her presentation by introducing her first song using a very marked Hispanic accent. She then sings the Spanish folk song, *Guantanamera.* Half way through the second verse she suddenly stops, puts her hand on one hip, looks directly out to the audience and, still using her accent, says, "But eef joo knew me a leetle betterr, joo wuld know dat summ of my faboreete museeik sounds like thees," and then she segues into a country western twang, plays her guitar and seductively sings, *Take the ribbon from 'mah' hair . . .* What she does in just a few minutes using music is to push the audience's emotional buttons to put them in touch with what may have been their initial prejudices. She then reminds them, "I'm the same person now that I was three minutes ago. You're just perceiving me differently."

7oasting a Master
DALE IRVIN

$\mathcal{D}$ale Irvin, CSP, CPAE, from Downers Grove, Illinois, is a stand-up comic and speaker who conducts workshops on developing humor. He also writes a humor newsletter called *Funny Business* (for a free sample, call 630-852-7695). Dale is a master at creating humor and offers a unique service to his clients, which he also provides at NSA conventions. At lunch during the convention, he supplies the audience with a "recap" of all the major sessions from the previous 24 hours. He takes a lot of notes during each general session and then creates topical humor based on what that speaker said earlier in the day. Obviously, this is very risky since there is no chance to try out any of the lines in front of an audience before the presentation. Yet this is one of the highlights of the convention.

One example of his approach was based on a speech given earlier that day by Tony Robbins. Dale said, "Now earlier today, Tony Robbins told us he once knew a woman who was scared of snakes. So to help her get over her fear of snakes, he brings her up on stage and gives her a . . . snake! Well, Tony, I haven't told anybody this, but, *Ferraris* scare the heck out of me!"

In Dale's humor workshops, he conducts several exercises for helping people learn how to develop humor. One technique is to read four or five newspapers every day. Look for articles that could make for funny lines, and then compare the material you write with the monologues on David Letterman and Jay Leno's shows that night. Once you start getting similar lines from time to time, you know you're on the right track. Another exercise is to take single panel cartoons from the paper and write your own captions.

Dale also says that you can learn a lot about the delivery of a line by listening to people tell jokes. Even if he's heard a joke a hundred times, he never stops the person from telling it because he might pick up a different nuance or approach to the joke that he didn't hear before.

Using Extemporaneous Humor

The most spontaneous and risky type of humor is ad-libbing or improvisational. It is also the most difficult and dangerous type of humor to develop. This usually occurs when you are reacting to someone in the audience or something happens in the meeting room. Some ad-libs can be used over again or can be developed for use when repeated opportunities happen. Perhaps during one of your speeches, a server drops a tray of dishes, everyone stares at someone in the front row who gets up and walks out, a fire alarm goes off, a phone, cell phone or beeper goes off, a baby cries, the mike goes out, you get feedback from the sound system, you sneeze or cough or any number of things.

You may wish to develop lines that you can use when these things happen. The line doesn't have to be super funny, but the reaction will be much greater since your line ties directly with something that happened right then and was unplanned. To get an idea of what many professional speakers do, pick up a copy of *What to Say When You're Dying on the Platform* (McGraw-Hill) by Lilly Walters. For example, in her chapter on "Antidotes to Audience Problems," there is a section entitled, ". . . They Yell, 'I Can't Hear You!'" One speaker, Ron Dentinger, was quoted as using the line, "There's a guy up front who says he can hear me just fine (pause) . . . and he'd like to switch seats with you."

A true ad-lib is a line you come up with, seemingly off the top of your head. This is also the most dangerous because the process is so fast that you often don't have time to make sure it's appropriate. Yet if you're capable of doing this kind of humor, it can add a tremendous advantage to your speaking. The people who regularly use this type of humor describe the process as being similar to a computer search. Someone in the audience asks a question that is different or unusual. Your brain starts searching the double meaning to set up the *misdirection.* If it can make the connection fast enough, the line will emerge immediately. So to be effective, the line has to not only be amusing but also delivered with timing.

It's difficult to give examples of this because they often don't make sense out of context or away from that particular audience. You've no doubt heard the cliché, "I guess you had to be there." That's true with this type of humor. Jeff uses a great deal of ad-lib humor in his workshops and seminars because there is a lot of interaction and questions with the participants. For example, when he was conducting a seminar on telephone selling techniques, a woman in the audience asked him, "What do you do when you keep getting answering machines?" Without missing a beat, he responded, "Well, you might call Radio Shack and get off their mailing list." It took a moment to sink in, then the audience started to laugh. Now, that line isn't super funny, but it got a better reaction than it deserved because it was obviously not planned and dealt with the question in an unusual way.

So how do you come up with a line like that? The audience member asked the question in such a way that it allowed for the interpretation. Obviously, she wanted to know what to do when you can't get your calls through to the person. "Getting answering machines" is the actual phrasing she used. Jeff then immediately saw the double meaning in the word "getting" and responded. She meant "getting" as "being connected to." Jeff used "getting" as "receiving," as in "receiving in the mail." Had she said, "What do you do when you keep getting voice mail?" or "What do you do when you have to leave a message?," the opportunity of coming up with an ad-lib would have changed.

Using Visual Humor

Even though you're speaking, you still have to give thought to the visual side of presenting humorous material. Assuming that the line is funny and you have the right timing to deliver it properly, you might also want to look at your facial expressions, gestures, body language and visual aids.

Though much about gestures and body language is covered in Chapter 5, props in Chapter 4, and visual aids in Chapter 6, you can break many of the rules (suggestions) when it comes to presenting something with humor. You might choose to overexaggerate certain gestures and your posture during a funny story to add more humor to your delivery. For example, Jeff tells a story about a six-year-old talking to her mother. Though he doesn't do an impression of their voices, he does look up and faces left when the six-year-old is talking to Mom, and he looks down and turns to the right when Mom answers the little girl. This role playing helps add to the humor of the words and timing of this story.

☞ Master's Tips:

1. *Once you have a funny line you use in your speech, look for ways to expand on it to get additional laughs.*
2. *Keep a journal of anything you see that you think is funny. Don't worry if it isn't relevant to your message yet, because it may be some day.*
3. *When someone tells you a joke that is "off color," see if you can rework it in some way so that it is still funny but not offensive.*
4. *Though your goal is not to become a comedian, consider visiting comedy clubs and watch comics on television. You can learn a lot from them. Though much of their humor is "off color," observe their sense of timing. Analyze why you think a certain line is funny. As an exercise, take a joke that bombs and see if you can rework it so it's funnier. Please remember that it's not ethical to use someone else's material in your speech without their permission. And lastly, if you think you have a funny line or improvement to a comic's routine, keep it to yourself. Most comics DON'T want suggestions from their audience.*

Chapter 4

*E*ngaging Effective Audience Participation

A powerful way to connect with and impact your audience is by involving them in your presentation. When you choose to use this kind of presentation technique, you evolve from the pure *keynote* mode into a *quasi-facilitator* mode. You are no longer merely lecturing; you are partnering with your audience.

Facilitators are clear on their objectives before they begin involving the audience. While not limited to longer presentations, audience participation is generally used more in the workshop or seminar format and less in the keynote address. Still, many excellent "keynoters" involve their audiences; this involvement ranges from the limited to the extensive.

Styles of Audience Participation Techniques

You can involve your audience in your presentation in many different ways. Here are some more commonly used approaches:

- the volunteer exercise
- the audience survey
- the individual question
- the partner exercise
- the small group exercise
- written exercises or note taking

The Volunteer Exercise

When you get a volunteer from the audience to help you with an exercise or demonstration, you also help to bring your entire audience into your presentation. Your audience members identify with that volunteer, especially if your volunteer is someone they know. At the same time, this process helps to bring you closer to your audience. If you're speaking on a platform or from behind a lectern, you have an opportunity to briefly "join" your audience by meeting your volunteer on the floor in front of the group.

As with any audience participation, you need a valid reason for using this technique. You should be reinforcing a point or helping to uncover some information that you need for your presentation.

The Audience Survey

Many speakers use this approach, which usually begins with, "By show of hands" or "By applause." Then the speaker asks a simple multiple choice question. This allows you to get a quick understanding of the needs or disposition of your audience. For example, when Jeff Slutsky is invited back to the same convention to present another breakout session on low-cost marketing and sales techniques, he needs to know how many people in the audience heard him the previous year. This is a valid concern because not all convention participants attend every year, and when they have a choice of three or four different sessions to attend, it's likely that many of his attendees have not heard him before. If that's the case, he can use his favorite fifteen-minute opener. If the majority have heard him before, he uses different material. In this way, he uses the audience survey to decide which material he covers.

The Individual Question

Many speakers, at different times during their presentations, ask their audience questions so that they can bring a list of ideas or problems out into the open. Then they present their speech based on these ideas. The key to this approach is that you know most, if not all, of the responses you're likely to get so that you give the same speech no matter what the audience provides. An example of this in a seminar on marketing would be when you say something like, "By show of hands, how many of you use direct mail advertising?" (count the hands). If only several hands go up, you may want to focus on a different kind of advertising.

A variation of the individual question is the question & answer or "Q & A" period, usually at the end of a presentation. This variation is different from the individual question not only because of its placement at the *end* of the presentation; in Q & A, the *audience,* not the speaker, asks the questions. The problem with Q & A is getting the audience started. Murray Raphael of Atlantic City, New Jersey, is a very talented speaker who suggests that if you're going to allow time for the audience to ask questions, you should plant at least five questions in the audience. Murray believes that audience members are reluctant to ask questions, but once those first questions are asked, the audience then feels more comfortable asking additional questions.

The Partner Exercise

The partner exercise requires the audience members to pair up with someone nearby. Depending on what you want them to accomplish through this technique, they can sit or stand. You then give your audience specific instructions on what you want them to do and how to do it. This is a perfect format for role-playing exercises, and you can combine it with your volunteer technique.

Jeff Slutsky does a partner exercise to get his audience going. About ten minutes into his keynote, he tells his audience that all the low-cost marketing, advertising, promotions and selling tactics that they're going to learn today are useless unless they treat their customers properly when they call or visit their business. Jeff tells them,

> To help illustrate this point, we're going to conduct an exercise that I usually do in a full-day seminar, but I thought I would try it here. This is something I want you to take back to your business and do with anyone in your organization who has direct customer contact. It will take only a minute. And in order for it to work, I need you to be perfectly silent. Now, without saying a word, I need everyone to stand up (everyone stands). Okay. Now, again without saying anything, face a partner, but be sure to be silent. You can do it in a small group of three if need be. Great. Okay. Here's the exercise. I'm going to count to

three. And when I reach three, I want you to look at your partner . . . then at the top of your lungs yell, "WHAT THE HELL DO YOU WANT?" ONE, TWO, THREE!

Everybody screams their heads off with this and laughs. Then Jeff responds with, "You guys have had practice at this one, haven't you?" Then he goes on, "Okay. Part 2 will probably be a little more difficult. This time I'm going to count to *three,* and when I reach three, I want you to look at your partner, and with your most sincere smile, and with your most sincere voice, say, 'Hi there. How can I be of service?' This may take five or six tries!"

This little exercise gets Jeff's audience laughing and helps set the mood and pace for the rest of the presentation.

Multiple participation tactics.   If you are teaching your participants a certain technique, such as how to handle an angry customer, for example, you could first bring up your volunteer and role play. Have your volunteer be your partner to play an angry customer. You respond to the volunteer's comments using the techniques you wish to teach to the audience. Once the demonstration is finished, you bring up another volunteer and have the partners role play in the same way. One of the two partners is selected to be the angry customer first, and the other partner uses the techniques to solve the problem. Then the roles are reversed.

When the exercise is completed, you can even add a third participation technique with a brief *audience survey* by asking the audience several specific questions about how they felt or what they learned from the role playing.

The Small Group Exercise

The small group approach to audience participation is best used for brainstorming sessions. This is where you want your participants to come up with solutions, suggestions, and even questions about a specific situation, problem, or opportunity.

You must stay in control.   The key to a successful small group exercise is to let your audience know what the rules are and how you'll conduct the session. It's too easy for these kinds of sessions to get out of control. You tell them when to begin and when to stop. You want to allot enough time for groups to come up with their lists of ideas, but not too much time because then they start discussing unrelated topics.

Set manageable group sizes.   You want your groups small enough so that everyone gets an opportunity to contribute, yet large enough to limit the number of groups to a manageable size. Generally, between four and eight is good. If your room is set up with *rounds,* that is, round tables that seat eight people, you might have one group per table. If you have control over the room setup and a small group exercise is a key element to your presentation, you may suggest that the meeting planner set the room with rounds.

Select a group leader.   You need to select, or have each group select, a team leader to serve as the team's spokesperson. This will make gathering the information much easier and more orderly. One of the simplest ways to gather the information is for you to go from table to table using a wireless handheld microphone. Then interview the team leader of each table. This keeps you in control because you have the mike. *Never* give the mike to anyone else. You also can have a volunteer list the group's suggestions on the overhead transparencies or a flip chart. Another advantage to using team leaders is that it gives you an opportunity to be in the audience, which helps you to establish a closer relationship with them.

Before you start circulating to get the suggestions, you may want to move from table to table (with the microphone muted) to see how each group is doing. You can even offer a suggestion, provide guidance, answer a question or simply compliment the group on their progress with the exercise. Each time you have one-on-one contact with audience members, you help to build greater rapport.

Written Exercises or Note Taking

A very easy way to get the audience to participate in your presentation is to ask them to take notes or complete written exercises. To get the most from these exercises, you may want to provide your attendees with a handout or workbook. These handouts help to focus them on the task and gives the participants something to take back with them after your presentation is over.

Toasting a Master
SCOTT FRIEDMAN

*W*hen it comes to involving his audiences, perhaps no one is better than Scott Friedman, a professional speaker based in Denver, Colorado, who, besides his main body of work, conducts special keynotes and seminars for singles groups. Scott combines nearly every audience participation technique in a single two-hour seminar. For example, he asks the question of the group, "What is your biggest 'pet peeve' about dating?" Then he encourages members of the audience to respond. Based on their responses, he composes a song (to the tune of the theme from the old comedy TV series, *The Beverly Hillbillies*) that he sings, accompanied by his guitar. He bases his lyrics on the pet peeves the audience provided. This reinforces the points the audience made and leads directly into helping the audience develop solutions later in his presentation.

Scott plants the seed.   To "prime the pump," Scott always tries to talk with some audience members before his presentation to get their response to that same question. Then if the audience is hesitant in shouting out their answers, he can call on one of the people he interviewed and say, "John and I were talking about this before the program, and he had an interesting thought. John?" With that encouragement, John then can mention what his concern about dating was. If John is still reluctant to speak, Scott can remind him what he said and simply get John to nod his head in agreement. This is usually enough to break the ice and get people to start giving their suggestions. Each suggestion can be written on an overhead transparency or flip chart. The audience's list is then used throughout the rest of the presentation.

With his experience, Scott has a good idea of what the answers are going to be. So he can even take an audience member's response, and by asking that person another question or two, he can guide that response into a format that Scott can more readily use in his presentation.

Written exercises can be serious, or they can be fun. In a goal-setting program, for example, you may ask your audience members to write down ten goals that they wish to accomplish in the next twelve months. Those ten goals will be specific to each audience member. Likewise, a financial planning seminar may ask the participant to list five long-term financial objectives. Writing down this information helps attendees learn about their needs and creates tangible records of their insights from your presentation. The completed handout or workbook becomes their personal guide to success.

Using quizzes and handouts. Spaced repetition learning is a teaching technique. If people hear something just once, they might get 10 percent of what you are saying. If they hear it and see it, retention jumps to 60 percent or more. If they see it, hear it and write it down, retention climbs to 85 percent or more. If they write it down and repeat it six times, retention climbs above 90 percent after a month.

Important material may have to be reinforced repeatedly to an audience. The trick is to find alternate ways to feed it to them. Quizzes work well because they allow you to test how you are doing with the audience. To make a quiz more fun, you could conduct it as a trivia contest with the answers coming from the key points of your presentation. Remember to reward good behavior by complimenting their efforts. Repeating this process again in longer programs allows you to reward many people and allows them to hear the message several times from several sources.

Fun written exercises. There are many written exercises and puzzles that you can incorporate into your presentation to get your audience more involved in the process. For example, Jeff and Marc Slutsky use a puzzle consisting of a box with nine dots to make a point about thinking beyond the normal boundaries. The goal is to connect all nine dots using only four straight consecutive lines. Do not repeat a line or lift your pen from the page. Hint: Think beyond the box. (See Figure 4.1.) For an even bigger challenge, do the same puzzle using only *three* lines. Hint: Think *way* beyond the box! The answers to the puzzles appear in Figures 4.3 and 4.4 at the end of this chapter.

FIGURE 4.1   Thinking Outside the Box

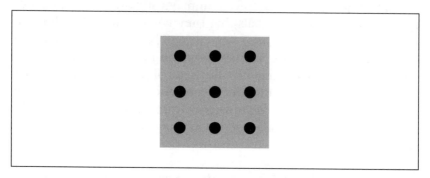

Avoiding Pitfalls of Audience Participation

Your presentation may benefit greatly from using some creative audience participation tactics, but you must be careful at the same time. Use these techniques properly so they don't backfire on you. First, make sure that your participation technique is relevant to your presentation. If you force a technique on the audience with no purpose or reason, you could lose credibility because your audience may feel that you're trying to manipulate them. When you use an exercise, share with the audience the reason for using it.

Another common occurrence when speakers use participation techniques is that some audience members will choose that time to leave the meeting room. One way to avoid this is to announce when the next break will be. Another way is by requesting that everyone stay to participate and if they need to leave, to do so after the exercise. Also, you want to make sure you have a specific amount of time for the exercise and that your audience knows that.

Audience Participation Exercises to Warm Up a Group

You can choose from endless variations of group exercises designed to involve an audience. Here are a few you might consider to warm up a group or to use as a bridge from another speaker or a Master of Ceremonies to your presentation.

Pat on the back.   If your group has had to endure a long-winded introduction (which should never happen but it does), you might have everyone raise their right hand into the air. "Now reach way over your shoulders," you say as you are showing them, "and give yourself a pat on the back for coming."

This always loosens the group up, and it becomes a good ice-breaker, especially if the speaker before you might have been boring or long winded.

Stand up and stretch break.   Again, if the circumstance dictates, consider a *stretch break* instead of a full break. Suppose the speaker ahead of you abused his or her time privilege and seriously cut into your time slot. Perhaps the audience has been there for some time and deserves a break, but you cannot afford to yield any more time.

The stand up and stretch break makes for an ideal compromise. Simply have everyone stand up in place, put their hands as far into the air as possible, stand on their tiptoes, ball their fists and stretch.

Another version of this is the *rubdown. You must be very careful to clear this with the meeting planner in advance.* Some groups are very sensitive about any kind of touching of other people. The rubdown is innocent enough. You have everyone turn in one direction, put their hands on the shoulders of the person in front of them and give them a shoulder rub. While this feels terrific, there is always someone who will take advantage of the situation or another who considers it a violation of their privacy. Be sure to clear it in advance.

The oxygen break.   Have everyone stand in place, take a deep breath and count to five. Then exhale. Take another deep breath and count to six. Then exhale. Take another deep breath and count to seven. Then exhale. This puts oxygen into the system, rushes it to the brain and helps everyone clear their heads. The exercise works well in an overheated or stuffy room.

The ice breaker.   Suppose you have a group of strangers or folks who perhaps know others only by name; the *icebreaker* works well. Have the first partner interview the second partner and list five facts about the first partner, which they report to the group. You do not have to interview the entire group. Call on a few to introduce the person next to them.

The mix master.   People tend to flock together with friends at meetings. Have your table (if you are in rounds) count off. Have all the one's go to table one, have all the two's go to table two, and so forth. This forces people to sit with strangers and get to know others at the meeting.

Simon says ...   Another method to get people moving around is to play a round of "Simon Says" with the group, moving those who goofed to another table or rewarding those who followed Simon's instructions with a choice of seating.

Plant rewards under seats.   To get people to sit toward the front of the room, some speakers plant rewards under the seats in the front rows. Dollar bills are great too. One speaker used to have everyone get off their seat to find the dollar bill taped underneath. Then he told them that the moral of this exercise is "You have to get off your butt to make a buck!"

The envelope please.   Each audience member gets an envelope, which contains a number. Since most round tables seat eight people, you fill eight envelopes with the number one, eight more envelopes with the number two, and so on until all envelopes contain a number in groups of eight. Shuffle the envelopes, and then pass them out to each audience member. For example, if you have 42 attendees, you don't want a table with only two people at it. So in this case, you would fill the envelopes with seven of each number.

Use any of these warm-up exercises when necessary. Each should accomplish a purpose. Do not fill the time with meaningless games. Use these methods as ways to get people involved and interacting with each other.

Discussion and Roleplaying Exercises

Huddle up.   In *huddle up*, our objective is to do just that. You might hold up a topic on a sign or overhead transparency.

Then ask the audience to break into groups of three or four and come up with 25 uses for the object or topic. Then say "Go!" and have them holler the answers back to you as you report the results on a flip chart or overhead transparency.

Brainstorming. *Brainstorming* is exactly what the word implies. You are looking for ideas that go beyond the basic topic itself. Let's assume the audience has experienced your presentation and now you want them to brainstorm to see what they can add to the subject.

You can tell your audience, "Take the next five minutes to turn to your neighbor and discuss the two best ideas you learned today and how you plan to apply them to your situation at work or home."

You can then call on several to share their ideas or simply send them home with a commitment to try the ideas they learned from the session.

The town reporter. Have them form circles of (you name the number) and count off. Have all the people who were number (you choose the number) act as group leaders. Ask the group leader to name a reporter to take notes to report to the general body. Present the topic, give them (you decide the amount of time) the time allotted for discussion, and ask the reporter to report the most important thing discussed in their group. If you have a sizable audience, do not let them offer more than one idea. This will give others a chance to participate. The reporter can work with a flip chart or an overhead transparency. Be sure to provide these at each table in advance, or have a microphone in place for the reporter to report to the facilitator, who will write down the information.

The devil's advocate. Have the audience members turn to their neighbor and take a few minutes to be *the devil's advocate* by coming up with concerns about carrying out the advice gained earlier. Have them complete the following sentence:

"I am concerned about doing _____
_____ because . . ."

"I am excited about doing _____

_____ because . . ."

Call on a few to share their concerns and excitement.

Team talk.   Team up in groups of (you choose the number) and elect a group leader. Tell the groups, "I would like you to identify the company that you feel does *(choose topic)* better than anyone else and tell why." You have five minutes. Team leaders will report the results back.

Or "I would like you to identify the things you want your (client, customer, audience member, friend) to perceive about you when your name/company is mentioned."

Or "I would like you to identify the areas about your (client, customer, audience member, friend) that you feel can be improved."

The list goes on and on. Using your creativity: you have no limit.

The Ben Franklin close.   Michael Aun likes to use the *Ben Franklin close* on large groups. Let's assume you have thousands of people in a convention center and you sincerely want audience opinions, but it is impossible to work the room with a microphone. Does that mean that you cannot solicit their opinion? Absolutely not.

Try using one of the oldest closing techniques around—affectionately named the Ben Franklin close. When faced with a dilemma, Ben Franklin would draw a T-diagram on a piece of paper. On one side, he would write the word "good," and on the other side, he would write the word "bad." He would then list the good reasons and the bad reasons about the subject under discussion.

Instead of "good" versus "bad," you could use words like "constructive" versus "destructive," "fulfilling" versus "frustrating," or "go" versus "no go." Be as creative as you want.

Have the group shout out their opinions and simply list them accordingly. This is a way of getting audience involvement and consensus without having hundreds of people report back as a whole. This works well when choices are clearly defined and limited.

Think like an attorney. Use questions that begin with the words "did," "would," "could," "should," "may"—questions that elicit a yes or no answer. When an attorney in a court of law asks a question, you can bet that he or she knows the answer as well as the next question. The key is not in the audience's answers but in how you ask your questions.

Debates.   A good old-fashioned debate is another great way to get the pros and cons of a topic in front of the group. They are a lot of fun and easy to pull off. You can even let the audience vote on their favorite position.

Sometimes it is easier to find proponents of a cause than opponents. You might select the participants and reverse the positions, making the proponent take the opposing view and vice versa. This forces the debaters to think on their feet and often brings out the best ideas.

Pantomimes.   The *pantomime* can be a lot of fun and can be done in many ways. Let's say you are speaking to a group of salespeople and you want to heighten their awareness about the concerns of their customers. Pair them off, then have one of them take on the role of an unruly customer, and let them share those concerns to the audience using pantomime. The other must deal with their silent customer's concerns also using pantomime. Once this is completed, have the two participants reverse roles and repeat the role-playing exercise.

Another form of role reversal is for managers to pantomime employees and employees to pantomime management. You must act as referee. Keep it fun and make your point in the process.

Another personality role Michael focuses on is the *coach* or *counselor*. This role gives people choices, which is the focus of the vignette. Of course, he has a hat that says "coach" on it.

Back-to-back communication.   An exercise Michael successfully uses with groups involves two audience members. They either come on stage or keep their positions in the audience. Have them sit back-to-back in their chairs, facing opposite directions. The exercise is on communicating. Give them both a piece of paper and have one give the other instructions.

The first time around, only the person giving instructions can speak. Have Party A instruct Party B on how to fold and tear the paper. Both parties tear and fold the paper simultaneously. The result should be two identically torn pieces of paper *if* Party A communicated correctly and Party B understood the communication.

Next, have Party B reverse the favor, but this time both parties openly communicate. When the communication is two-way, generally the parties end with perfectly matched tears in their paper.

You can even do this exercise with your audience, having them give you folding and tearing instructions or you issuing the instructions.

Using Props to Get Participation

Sometimes props can be effective tools to encourage audience participation. Let's look at some examples.

Bouncing balls and frisbees.   One way to pass the baton to someone else is by using a beach ball and passing it around the room. Whoever catches it offers an idea and tosses the ball to the next person. Frisbees work just as well. This helps recapture the thoughts discussed over the course of the day. You can adapt this in dozens of ways, depending on the size of the group and how much participation you are seeking.

Using props in skits.   Michael particularly enjoys putting on skits that involve using audience members to make important points. One of his favorite topics is about management and leadership styles. He tells a humorous story about "helicopters, drill sergeants and coaches," three management styles that he identifies with hats that high-profile audience members wear on the platform. The "helicopter" wears a little beanie, purchased from Universal Studios in Orlando, that has a little propeller on top. Michael has several versions of these, so he generally pulls at least two audience members on the stage to wear those hats. Another version of the helicopter style is the "rescuer" personality. He has an audience member don a rescuer prop, a fire fighter's hat.

The drill sergeant wears an Army helmet or a drill instructor's hat, both of which he happens to have in his arsenal. It is usually easy to find the drill sergeant types in an audience, and his helpers have loads of fun with them on the stage.

Props are a great way to involve an audience. The audience members need not know a script, although they often know the answers. For instance, the Drill Sergeant always says "it's my way

FIGURE 4.2   Sometimes a Little Magic Involves Your Audience

16	29	58	87
17	30	59	88
18	31	60	89
19	48	61	90
20	49	62	91
21	50	63	92
22	51	80	93
23	52	81	94
24	53	82	95
25	54	83	
26	55	84	
27	56	85	
28	57	86	

or . . . " They finish the line . . . "the highway." Or, some might say . . . "it's my way or else . . . " or "it's my way or NO way . . . " The result is the same. Always make them the stars of the show and do not be afraid to involve them.

Magic tricks.   For some time now, Michael has been wanting to involve some magic into his own presentations, but he wanted the magic to have a point. So he went to his friend, "The Great Hondo!" of Minneapolis. Since Michael does a lot of speaking to his salespeople and to sales groups in general, he told Hondo that he needed some magic to help him make the point that, as salespeople, we know what clients are going to say before they say it . . . if we ask the right questions and read their body language.

Hondo introduced Michael to a simple piece of magic that involves Michael pulling two people onto the stage. Michael asks Party A to think of a number between 1 and 100. Then Party A tells Party B the number privately. Michael gives seven cards to Party A and asks Party A to remove all the cards on which the chosen number appears. Michael then tells Party A the number by adding up the numbers in the top left corner of the remaining cards. It always works and the audience loves it. (See Figure 4.2 for an example of one of the seven cards.)

Michael Aun is not likely to be the next "Hondo," nor is he interested in taking the place of the Amazing Kreskin, the great Gil Eagles or Shep Hyken or any other great speaker who uses magic. He has worked with all these great talents and admires and respects them for what they do. He does not want to be a magician, but it does not preclude him from working one or two pieces of "meaningful magic" into his presentation to make a point.

A great resource for incorporating magic into your presentation is a series of 3 videos entitled *Tricks for Trainers,* featuring Dave Arch, that is available through Smart Choice Media (800-294-1140). This video series not only teaches you some simple magic tricks but also how to reinforce a point in your presentation.

Bells, whistles, kazoos, and more props.   Audience participation can come in other forms as well. Michael uses whistles and bells in a variety of ways, from stopping a long-winded participant to starting a session. He even has a siren, which he stole from his son, Christopher, that blows four different kinds of whistles. His son is still searching for his bicycle-mounted siren. When you have audience involvement and you need to get attention, these devices are fun to work with, but make no mistake about it: They do not replace the message. The messenger must still deliver.

Michael even has a little squawk box that simulates bombs going off. He hasn't quite figured out how to incorporate this gadget yet, but rest assured, you will see it in some future presentation.

☞ Master's Tip:

- *Plan! Plan! Plan! Nothing just happens. If you want someone to ask questions, pick out a special, high-profile person, and make sure they have a good question to ask. If not, give them one. Then reward them for participating.*
- *Stick to your main purpose. Make sure that your participation techniques reinforce your message, not distract from it.*
- *Stay in charge. It is easy to let the program manage you rather than you manage the program. Learn when to say no, and "don't beat a dead horse," as Rosita Perez, CSP, CPAE, would advise. Know when to give up the hunt. Some things just do not work. Do not force them.*

- **Let your audience take pride and ownership in their participation.** *If you are trying to convey certain ideas that will make your audience better at a particular thing, they will buy into it a lot quicker if they feel it is their idea and not yours.*
- **Know that most people are terrified to speak in front of others.** *Do not bully these folks into this process. Try to identify them in advance through the meeting planner, and avoid putting them on the spot. You do not want to embarrass anyone.*

FIGURE 4.3   You Solve the Puzzle by "Thinking Outside the Box"

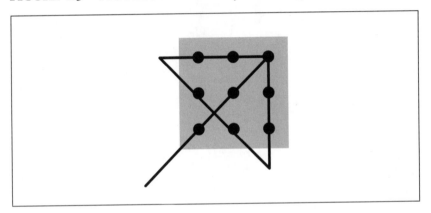

FIGURE 4.4   You Solve the Puzzle by "Thinking *Way* Outside the Box"!

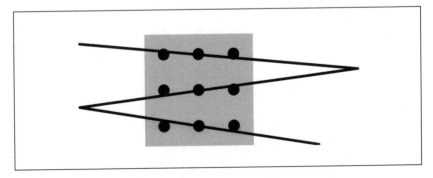

Chapter 5

Developing Your Gestures, Body Language, Voice Modulation, and Vocal Variety

A problem for many speakers is that they are too mechanical in their presentations. Often, they take on the appearance of a robot going through preprogrammed, lifeless motions. Not only do you want to immediately capture the attention of your audience with your words and voice; you also want to create sincerity with your gestures and body movement.

It is too easy to lose an audience in the first few minutes of a presentation, which is why you must grasp their attention right away. Overdramatizing your presentation with exaggerated gestures can turn off your audience. Conversely, a deadpan presentation with little or no movement or gestures can kill the audience just as quickly. Consider the various techniques you can employ to improve your audience's acceptance of your presentation.

In this chapter, you will be introduced to four important tools for making strong speeches: gestures, body language, voice modulation and vocal variety.

Getting the Most from Your Gestures

Gestures are most effective when they're appropriate to the unique circumstances of your presentation. Gestures can serve as visual punctuation to underscore your message so your audience fully understands your meaning. It is best to let the event and the audience dictate the amount of gesturing you should do. If you are detailing three points, for example, you might show the audience the number of the point you are on with your fingers. So as you say, "My first point is . . . ," you would use a "number one" gesture. That's appropriate.

Benefits of Gestures

Toastmasters International says that "gestures are probably the most evocative form of nonverbal communication a speaker can employ. No other kind of physical action can enhance your speeches in as many ways as gestures can." *Gestures: Your Body Speaks,* a manual available through Toastmasters, offers the following seven benefits of integrating gestures in your speech:

1.   They clarify and support your words.
2.   They dramatize your ideas.
3.   They lend emphasis and vitality to the spoken word.
4.   They help dissipate nervous tension.
5.   They function as visual aids.
6.   They stimulate audience participation.
7.   They are highly visible.

Avoiding Improper Use of Gestures

When your gestures conflict with your words, you send mixed signals to your audience, which can cause you to lose credibility and rapport. A gesture might be inappropriate when a speaker makes a gesture to try to create some drama in the presentation and it just doesn't work. This could be moving an arm out to the side or out and up at a 45 degree angle from the body during a point in the speech, but that gesture might not make sense for that particular message. It looks too contrived and unnecessary.

Most gestures for speaking are done with the arms, but using the head and even the entire body can be effective. One example might be when you are telling a story about two people talking. Instead of merely relating the story, you recreate the dialogue playing both parts. When the first person is talking, you turn your head to the right. When the second person is talking, you turn your head to left. These movements help you re-create the event for your audience and, if done right, make your story more entertaining. However, you should take into consideration several conditions of your speech when weaving gestures into the presentation. These include

- room size
- audience size
- focus of the event or presentation
- distance from the speaker to the audience
- sound system and acoustics of the meeting room

Adapt your gestures to the audience and room size. If you are speaking in a room where an audience is small enough that no microphone is needed, you might want to de-emphasize your gestures somewhat. The absence of a sound system might require more attention to vocal impact than to movement or gestures. You should arrive early to review the size and layout of the meeting room. If you're preceded by other speakers, go to the back of the room, watch their movements, and listen to how well they are being heard and listened to by the audience.

For instance, in a smaller, more intimate gathering where you don't need or don't have a microphone, you might want to keep most of your gestures closer to the body, above the waist, and below the shoulders. Conversely, in a larger audience you would need to exaggerate those same gestures to make an impact with the audience. If the group is large enough, it would be appropriate to gesture above your head or way out to the side of your body. The exception is if the auditorium is so large that your presentation is being projected on a large screen. Then you can rein in your gestures to a more intimate level.

Some politicians are terrific orators while others have a penchant for overkill, especially in this area. When Michael Aun ran for the House of Representatives, he watched many politicians make their pitch. Because a festival was going on in South Carolina almost every weekend of the month, these events always took place around a down home, mustard-based, barbeque pork roast in the dead heat of summer.

In the small town of Gilbert at the Lexington County Peach Festival, Michael heard one of the finest speakers ever to take the platform. Tom Turnipseed, who was running for governor, was not only a tremendous orator; he could also command a presence from a platform by using some powerful gestures. For instance, he would pound on the lectern and stomp around the podium to emphasize his points. Most of those presentations were generally outside, and many times very poor or no sound systems were available.

Later, Michael and Tom both spoke at a Rotary Club program. During Tom's presentation, his content was fundamentally the same, but his gesturing was less volatile. For this presentation, he was speaking inside a restaurant with an excellent sound system, so he didn't need to shout to be heard. Furthermore, he had to speak behind a lectern and was limited physically to the immediate area around it.

Tom adjusted magnificently. Instead of roaming around the podium, he pounded on the lectern to make his major points. Instead of raising his voice to stress important issues, he would lower it to a whisper, magnifying his presence as the listener would lean forward to hear what he had to say. Most importantly, he restrained his gestures. Inside the restaurant, he kept his gestures above the lectern and within a foot or so of both sides of his body. At other times when speaking outside on the back of a flatbed truck, he moved frequently, pounding the podium and hammering on the lectern to emphasize his points in evangelical style. When outside, he waved his arms as he hollered out his theme "Fool Yourselves." Inside, he merely pointed to different members of the audience, locking in with eye contact, to make the same point. Tom brilliantly adapted his gestures to the occasion and the forum.

In the late 1970s and early 1980s, Michael spoke at a number of "Positive Thinking Rallies" held in huge arenas accommodating thousands of people. In the Charlotte Coliseum in 1979, the program headliners included Paul Harvey, the late Dr. Norman Vincent Peale, the late Ira Hayes and Ty Boyd. When speaking in huge arenas like the Charlotte Coliseum, you have to overexaggerate your gestures so that you can make an impact even with those people to whom you are no more than a dot on a stage several hundred feet away. In this size arena, with this type of audience and message, it is appropriate to run back and forth, wave your arms, kneel, or do whatever feels right.

Zig Ziglar hit his knee in a semi-crouch as if to bend down to be closer to his audience. In a format such as that area, almost any and all movement is acceptable, except movement off the stage. Generally, the lighting in the aisles is not as good, so that kind of body language is more harmful than helpful.

Jeff Slutsky had a similar experience when speaking in Singapore and Kuala Lampur at a sales rally kicked off by Tom Hopkins, one of the best known sales trainers in the world. The audiences were over 5,500 and 4,500, respectively, but since the speaker were projected on larger-than-life TV screens, they adjusted their movements and gestures as if they were speaking before a more intimate audience. Your movement should be less exaggerated when a camera is closely focused on your upper body. Any volatile or hasty movement might move you "out of the picture" before the camera operator can adjust.

Restraint is the order of the day when video is involved. Make sure that your facial expressions are appropriate as well. In a huge chamber like the Superdome, for example, facial expressions mean nothing if there is no video to magnify your image to the conclave. Throw in the cameras and you have a whole new environment to which you must adjust.

Toastmasters International's Six Tips for Effective Gesturing

Here are six tips Toastmasters International suggests to help you use your gestures more effectively:

1. Respond naturally to what you think, feel, and say.
2. Create the conditions for gesturing, not the gesture.
3. Suit the action to the word and the occasion.
4. Make the gestures convincing.
5. Make your gestures smooth and well timed.
6. Make natural, spontaneous gesturing a habit.

Gestures to Avoid or Minimize

Certain kinds of gestures have a tendency to be too contrived or cliché. Some of the more obvious ones to avoid include the following:

- The *fig leaf* gesture, where you hold your hands together in front of your body near your abdomen.
- The *pledge of allegiance* gesture, where you hold your hand over your heart as if you are pledging to the flag.
- The *praying hands* gesture, where you clasp your hands together as if you are praying.
- The *scratching head* gesture, as if you are scratching something that itches or searching for some magical information.
- The *mobster* gesture, where you look to be reaching inside your coat pocket to pull out your gun.
- The *body part pull,* where you pull on various body parts, such as the nose, ears, chin or other areas.
- The *hands in the pocket* gesture, as if you are too cold to keep them out.
- The *Statue of Liberty* gesture, which looks contrived because you are standing there holding your hand upright for no particular reason.
- The *wand waving* gesture, where you give that sweeping wave that looks staged.
- The *machine gun* gesture, where you repeatedly point at someone or something as if your machine gun is mowing them down.

Toastmasters International considers proper gestures to be so important that the organization devoted an entire manual to the topic: *Gestures: Your Body Speaks.* In this valuable manual, you learn that often the body speaks louder than the words. Toastmasters International says:

> When you present a speech, you send two kinds of messages to your audience. While your voice is transmitting a verbal message, a vast amount of information is being visually conveyed by your appearance, your manner, and your physical behavior.

The old expression "actions speak louder than words" is true in speaking if the actions overshadow the words. But your speech will be more effective if your actions reinforce the words. As Ralph Waldo Emerson said, "What you are speaks so loudly that I cannot hear what you are saying." In other words, if you are not earnest and sincere, your body language and gestures will betray you.

Making Use of Body Language

While gestures usually involve the way you use your hands and arms, body language refers more to your posture or carriage. Your body language says a lot about your confidence. If, for example, you are slumping on the platform, the audience might perceive you as indifferent, bored or uneasy. Too much movement on the platform, though, exudes nervousness or ambivalence.

Body language is as much about your physical makeup as it is about the image you are trying to portray. Body language is also about the way you are dressed. Body language can help with the persuasion process. Toastmasters International devotes an entire speech assignment to what it calls "Persuade with Power." While the objectives of that assignment have their foundation in the body and content of the speech, body language can and does have as much to do with the audience's reception of your remarks. Toastmasters gives us three solid benefits of effective physical action on the platform:

1. It makes your messages more meaningful and memorable.
2. It adds punctuation to your speeches.
3. It helps relieve your nervous tension.

Making Greater Impact with Proper Body Language

Building a rapport with your audience is always very challenging. Using your body language properly can help you overcome that challenge so that your audience gives you a fair shot at presenting your message. Here are five helpful tips from Toastmasters International:

Rid yourself of distracting mannerisms.   Dr. Ralph C. Smedley, the founder of Toastmasters International, wrote, "The speaker who stands and talks at ease is the one who can be heard without weariness. If his posture and gestures are so graceful and unobtrusive that no one notices them, he may be counted truly successful."

Dale Carnegie, the father of modern public speaking, said that the problem of learning effective speech delivery is not one of superimposing additional characteristics; rather; it is one of removing impediments.

Be natural, spontaneous, and conversational. Don't try to imitate another speaker. Instead, let yourself respond naturally and spontaneously to what you think, feel, and say. Strive to be as genuine and natural as when you talk informally with friends or family. And as funny as it may sound, you actually have to practice being spontaneous.

Today's speaking style can best be described as "enlarged conversation." It's much more informal than the pompous, oratorical style that characterized public speaking in years past. The emphasis is on communication and sharing ideas, not on performance or sermonizing.

Let your body mirror your feelings. As Dale Carnegie wrote, "A person under the influence of his feelings projects the real self, acting naturally and spontaneously. A speaker who is interested will usually be interesting."

Build self-confidence through preparation. Nothing influences a speaker's mental attitude more than the knowledge that he or she is thoroughly prepared. This knowledge is expressed by self-confidence, which is a vital ingredient of effective public speaking.

Use Your Toastmasters International Club as a Learning Laboratory

The key to improving your performance in any endeavor is to practice. Your local Toastmasters International club offers you a hands-on workshop where you'll gain valuable experience. It's a place where mistakes cost you nothing and the audience is always patient, supportive, and helpful. It is true . . . "practice makes perfect." What is even more accurate is "perfect practice makes perfect." You don't have to compete if you don't want to, but it is another opportunity to fine-tune your presentation skills. When Michael Aun won the World Championship of Public Speaking for Toastmasters International in 1978 in Vancouver, British Columbia, he practiced the winning speech at least 300 times over the course of about 30 days.

The World Championship competition requires that every speech from the District level on up be a new and different presentation from any and all previous presentations. In fact, you must provide Toastmasters International written copies of all your previous speeches so that there is no noticeable duplication of material. You do not have the luxury of writing one super speech to carry the day.

That means that you are constantly developing new material, and the time frame between these competitions narrows the further you advance through the process. It happened that Michael won the Regional contest in Norfolk, Virginia, and had about 30 days to get ready for the International finals in Vancouver. During those 30 days, he gave his speech in the shower, in the car, to friends, at Toastmasters International clubs, to civic clubs, to his wife, and even to his dog. If anybody or anything would listen, he gave them that speech. He was determined not to let the disaster of the previous year take him down again (when he went eight seconds over time in Toronto, Ontario). Not only did he get proficient at the presentation, but he also noticed that the more he presented his speech, the more comfortable he felt with his body language and gestures.

Body Language beyond the Lectern

Most professional speakers don't stand behind a lectern. Many even venture into the audience, taking full advantage of their own body movement to help their audience become more involved in their presentation. Jeff Slutsky, when presenting his keynote speech, *Confessions of a Street Fighter,* asks for a volunteer for a little exercise about five minutes into his speech. For the first several minutes, he shares with the audience just how much advertising and marketing are ignored. He claims that most of the money spent on advertising is wasted. To prove his point, the volunteer comes forward, and Jeff meets him or her in front of the stage. He then gives that person 20 seconds to name 25 brands of laundry detergent as quickly as possible. Generally, that volunteer will be hard pressed to name two or three even though the soap companies spend billions of dollars to keep their brand names on top of everybody's mind.

Not only does this exercise prove a point, but it also gives Jeff a reason to move into the audience briefly and establish greater rapport. When the exercise is over, he's back on stage, and everyone gives the volunteer a hand for helping out.

Voice Modulation and Vocal Variety

Fred Wienecke and Sonny Dixon were two of the tremendous speakers Michael competed against on the road to the World Championship of Public Speaking. Fred's strength came from the way he used his voice. To make powerful points, he would lower his voice to a whisper. In Vancouver that year, he whispered the closing words, "Never give up, never, never, never give up."

Sonny Dixon brought another kind of vocal power to his presentation the first year Michael competed against him in the Regional in Jekyll Island, Georgia. Sonny was a broadcaster by profession and knew the power of imitation and voice modulation. He could make his voice climb to a peak and drop to a whisper, all in the same sentence. What gestures are to your physical appearance, effective voice modulation and vocal variety is to your content. Nothing can kill a presentation quicker than using powerful words in a dull and unconvincing manner. To help you improve, record your voice and listen to it. Then practice, practice, practice.

If possible, record your presentations on video so you can evaluate your gestures and body language as well as your voice. You can be your own best speech coach. Sometimes you merely have to see and hear what you're doing, and you can easily correct any problem.

The best way to test your vocal variety and voice modulation, though, is to try it out in a format where you respect the opinions of your listeners. If your audience receives your material as you intended, you have a keeper.

If you did not get the response you had hoped for, go back to the drawing board to see if your method of delivery might have had more to do with the reception of the speech than the material itself.

Dorothy Leeds, an accomplished speaker and author of *Smart Questions,* does an exercise in her seminars where she has her participants each read a passage from the children's book *Green Eggs and Ham,* by Dr. Seuss. Each person is told to read using a certain emotion like angry, surprised, happy, sad, and so on. By changing their emotion, the same words sounded totally different. Dorothy is convinced that some people could stand up and read the telephone book and make it sound interesting; others could deliver Lincoln's Gettysburg Address and slaughter it beyond recognition. The difference is in the delivery, and that is as much about vocal variety and voice modulation as it is about content.

The great orators of yesterday, like the Abraham Lincolns, had to depend on superior oratorical skills to make their points. They did not have the benefit of sound systems and audiovisual aids. They were their own props. Unlike Lincoln, we live in a highly visual society today, and though great orators are still respected, they are being upstaged by speakers with tremendous audiovisual aids and other tools that are now the standard for the profession of public speaking.

Other People's Feedback

To make sure that your gestures, body language, and voice are helping you maximize your impact from the platform, get feedback from people you care about and who care about you. A mentor will tell you what you are doing right and what you are doing wrong. However, when asking friends for their comments be sure that what you get is useful. For example, when asking someone to give you their thoughts about elements of your presentation, make sure that they know that you want their opinions about your presentation style, not the content.

Michael's grandfather taught him years ago to "listen to the criticism of others, but do not necessarily support them." He added, "There is no such thing as constructive criticism. Most criticism is destructive because more often than not, the person doing the criticizing is criticizing the performer and not the performance." Something is inherently wrong in that kind of criticism.

Look for a mentor who will respect you enough to tell you what you are doing right as well as what you are doing wrong. Most of us join an organization like Toastmasters International because we are not comfortable with our skills and we fear the platform. With egos this fragile, you do not need people who will hamper your enthusiasm. On the other hand, you do not need people who will "whitewash" you either. Seek out honest, forthright feedback, but keep it in context.

☞ **Master's Tip:** *Giving a speech is both verbal and visual so incorporate appropriate gestures and movements into your presentation.*

Chapter 6

*I*ncorporating Visual Aids to Enhance Your Presentations

*V*isual aids can be powerful tools for effective communication. Toastmasters International encourages their use but only when they enhance a speech. When you use visual aids correctly in your presentations, you can reap many benefits.

Benefits of Using Visual Aids

- Increase your audience's comprehension of your message.
- Increase your audience's retention of your message.
- Increase the speed at which your audience understands your message.
- Enhance attention from your audience.
- Keep your presentation on track.
- Control your nervousness.

According to research conducted by Michael Aun, if you simply stand up and give a speech, the audience is lucky if they retain 10 percent of what you have to say from the platform. However, if you use visuals, such as slides, overheads, props, video, and other support material, retention leaps to 60 percent or more. Furthermore, when you provide a handout, retention rockets to 85 percent provided that the audience reviews the handout at least once.

Visual aids range from simple hand-held objects to expensive multimedia extravaganzas. According to Toastmasters International, your choice for a particular speech depends on several factors:

- the information you wish to convey
- the size of the audience
- the equipment available to you
- the time available to prepare the visual
- the amount of money you wish to spend

Disadvantages of Using Visuals

There is also a downside to using visual aids. You have to transport them when you travel. You have to keep your visuals in topnotch condition. But perhaps the biggest challenge with all forms of audiovisual aids is that you increase the chances of a technical glitch that could adversely impact your presentation. The more you rely on technology in your presentation, the more you are at risk. So whenever you use any form of technology in your presentation, make sure you are extremely comfortable with it before you bring it to the platform. You also should have contingency plans to deal with problems that may occur, including the ability to deliver your presentation without the use of audiovisuals if necessary.

To avoid these potential problems and maximize the effectiveness of your presentation, Toastmasters International suggests that every speaker who wants to use visual aids must adhere to the following two rules:

1. *Make visual aids visible.* "When preparing visuals, make large letters. A good rule of thumb is one-half inch for each ten feet between the visual and the farthest audience member. Print neatly, keep lines horizontal, and use plenty of spacing between the words. Display your visuals high enough so all can see, and avoid standing in front of them. Test visibility by viewing your visuals from various spots in the room before your speech."

2. *Keep visual aids simple.* "Use a simple visual aid to illustrate a single point. Make graphs and diagrams simple and accurate, giving each a title and labeling key components. With writing, follow the 'seven-seven rule': No more than seven lines and no more than seven words per line."

*T*oasting a *M*aster
IRA HAYES, CPAE

*T*he late Ira Hayes was the master of all masters at using one of the very first forms of visual aids: signs. What Ira used to do from the platform was the envy of every speaker in his day. For over 40 years, Ira delivered the same identical speech, first as a hired gun for his company, National Cash Register, and later as a keynote speaker.

Ira Hayes blew audiences away with his wit, wisdom, and engaging charm, which was reinforced by his great use of signs as props in his speech. Ira got his start in the speaking profession before it was common to see a lot of audiovisual support on the platform. He said, "I've been speaking so long that I remember when microphones were introduced to the speaking profession."

In the early days of his career, audiovisual devices like slide projectors, film, and overheads were just not that common, so Ira created his own "low-tech" visuals that were very effective for him.

As the new technology began to emerge in the forms of slide projectors and overhead projectors, Ira chose to stay with the slightly more burdensome signs that had worked well for him for over 40 years. He once commented that he didn't convert to slides or some other form of visuals because, "I am the only guy in America who uses these props. Why would I want to change that?" In that way, Ira's use of the old form of visuals later in his career made him unique in his marketplace.

Types of Visual Aids

You have a wide variety of visual aids that you can use to enhance your presentation. The visual media you choose for your presentation depends on your type of program, audience and meeting room. The most common visual aids include the following:

- flip charts
- transparencies and overhead projectors
- 35 mm slides and projector

- computer presentation software and video projector
- prerecorded videotape and monitors or video projector
- props

Each of these types of visual aid media allows you to prepare the visuals in advance of your presentation. However, of those listed above, only flip charts and transparencies allow you the additional benefit of creating the visual as you're speaking. This is often used with the audience participation segment of your talk where your group offers ideas. Chalk boards and white boards, though generally not used as much as those listed above, are exclusively used for creating the visuals while you present your material.

Flip Charts

Flip charts are a terrific communication medium, especially for a small group. They are inexpensive and generally available at most meeting places. Plus you can even use them in large groups where you are being projected on large TV screens. One screen can focus mainly on you, and the other on the flip chart or other visuals. If you are writing or illustrating with a flip chart as you speak before your audience, remember that *you,* not the chart, are still the main focal point.

If you are working with material that you produced prior to the program, then you want to make the appearance of pages as professional as possible. The audience does not have the luxury of watching the material unfold because it is already written. Now you, the speaker, must bring life to it.

Limit the Number of Words or Elements Per Page

The first key to this process is to limit the number of words per page on your flip chart, using only those words that reinforce the point you're making. Writing every detail on your flip chart makes it more difficult for your audience to understand your key points. The fewer the number of words or illustrations on the page, within reason, the more your audience is likely to remember because you place more importance on those particular words and fewer words are easier to recall. Plus when writing on the chart during your presentation, you don't needlessly bore your audience by having them watch you write more than you talk.

Write and Illustrate Legibly and Precisely

Your audience has to be able to understand what you've presented on your flip chart, so make sure you that write clearly. If what you're writing causes you to rush, you may want to practice using a flip chart so that you can write fast and yet still write legibly. The same idea applies to your illustrations. If you're not a particularly good artist, it's a good idea to practice the illustrations that you frequently use on your flip charts. Practice to the point where you can draw your illustrations exactly the way you want with a fair amount of speed. If you have time before your presentation, you can predraw your illustrations very lightly with pencil so that only you can see them. Then you simply trace over the pencil with a colored marker.

If you are going to use artwork, avoid stick figures unless you are doing it live. If you are preparing it in advance, the same meticulous care that would go into preparing a sign, slide, or transparency should go into the flip chart.

Use large block letters. You may want to outline the letter in black and color in the interior with a color like red, yellow, or green. Bright colors also might help to burn those ideas into the minds of your audience members.

Sequential Charts

When working with a sequence of visuals on a flip chart, remember to skip pages and tape the edge of the page just before your next visual. By attaching a piece of masking tape with a sequential number or letter written on it, you know where to flip to get to the next image. By attaching this tape to the page before the image, you know that when you flip over that page, your image page will appear. Consider staggering these pieces of tape up and down one side of the page in order of progression, like the tabs on a notebook. This makes your illustrations easy to find and get to so your audience does not have to wait.

When preparing the visual itself, remember to save yourself a big enough blank area on the sheet if you plan to add to the visual during the presentation. For example, if you want to stress five key points to remember about a particular topic (i.e., GOALS), the topic might appear at the top with the key points outlined below. (See Figure 6.1.) These key points can then be written in as you present them. The best part about using flip charts is the spontaneity of the situation. You can be very creative in the process. It also helps lend itself to audience participation. (See Chapter 8.)

Window Charts

Another unique way to use a flip chart is a concept called *windowing.* Bob Pike, CSP, a speaker, trainer and member of the National Speakers Association, uses windowing with his flip charts very effectively. He taught Michael Aun an interesting way of incorporating this flip chart technique for illustrating a story he tells about leadership styles. He makes several points, all of which surround the word "CHOICES" during this vignette.

To do this, Bob first decided how many separate visuals he wanted to use surrounding the word. To use the word "CHOICES" in three separate visuals, you would need nine sheets on the flip chart. This gives you three blank pages between each of the three pages to prevent the next image from bleeding through onto the current image. You might also want to leave the first three pages blank before the first illustration to use the element of surprise when you begin the vignette. To do this, you need a total of 12 pages.

Next, on the twelfth page, you write the word "CHOICES" in big, bold block letters that can be enhanced with different colored markers if you choose. Then flip the 11 previous pages over, several pages at a time, and use an X-acto knife to cut a window in the pages before the word *page,* so that "CHOICES" shows through the windows. Be careful to put some cardboard behind the pages being cut so that you do not cut the page on which your "window word" appears. Also, use a straight edge so the cut lines are clean and straight. Make sure the window is consistent as well. You can trace in a cut line if you have trouble guessing where it should go.

Now you have a total of some 12 pages, 11 of which have a window in them with the twelfth page showing the word "CHOICES" through each window. Remember to use your masking tape on the

FIGURE 6.1   Sample Flip Chart Page

FIVE POINTS
TO REMEMBER
ABOUT GOALS

1. _____

2. _____

3. _____

4. _____

5. _____

edge to mark your next sequence page and also to mark the page prior to your actual image page. Now you can add the three "types" of CHOICES you wish to address on each of the three pages.

When possible, produce the pages in advance and tailor the message for the company's or association's name along with jargon that is specific to the group. Also, you may want to save plenty of white space as well as "window pages" between the images to allow for an ad-lib if you desire.

Story Boarding with Flip Charts

Another technique that is often used for meetings where there is a lot of idea development and participation from the audience is *story boarding*. The audience is divided into a number of small groups of, say, four to eight. The speaker gives the different groups problems to solve or situations that require some kind of idea development. As they begin to come up with their ideas or solutions, they put them down on their own flip chart. Then these pages are taped to the surrounding walls for all to see. Each team presents their ideas to the rest of the group, with the speaker serving as the moderator.

Transparencies and Overhead Projectors

Overhead transparency equipment is easily available and relatively inexpensive, so most meeting places can provide one for you; however, some may charge a fee for their use. As a Field Agent with the Knights of Columbus Insurance, Michael found it necessary to own a "briefcase" style overhead transparency machine, which he still uses today. Because the wattage is minimal, it cannot be used for a huge group of people, but it is adequate for any group under 50.

Michael even found it useful to take it into a home and put it on the kitchen table when speaking to several people and simply flash the image on the wall. In a formal speaking environment, all you need is a white or clear wall or a screen and you are in business. The advantage of the overhead, or *acetate* as they are sometimes called, is that you can easily maintain eye contact with your audience while you refer to the image on the screen because you are facing the audience when using it. A flip chart, on the other hand, requires you to turn your back to the audience.

You can also write on the overhead to reinforce or make additional points that are not already on it. By using a simple felt tip pen, you can also point to items you would like to emphasize without standing in front of the screen.

A wide range of overheads are available today from computer-generated transparencies to those you could run through the bypass of a copy machine. You can use both bordered and nonbordered transparencies. The advantage of the bordered transparency is that you can make notes to yourself on the border that you might not want on the overhead itself. Another advantage is that it gives the image a neat appearance on the screen.

The nonbordered transparency is less expensive. If you plan to reuse the transparency, you might want to use the nonbordered, black and white style. Since transparencies are available in multiple colors, cost can vary. You can also attach these nonbordered transparencies to a cardboard border, thus creating the outside border for one-time use.

Transparencies can be produced on a photocopy machine or directly from a laser printer. This allows you to replicate your handout material and project it on the screen for the audience. Anything that can be photocopied can be put on the transparency.

You can even produce black and white or color (if you have a color printer/copier) transparencies of support material or examples you wish to share with the audience. For example, if you're talking about an event that received a great deal of press coverage, you can duplicate the press clippings on the transparency. Of course, the quality of the transparency is only as good as the copier or printer that you use.

Great Flexibility

In addition to keeping eye contact with your audience, another advantage over more structured forms of visuals like 35 mm slides is that you can select only those transparencies you want at that moment. If your audience's needs are moving your presentation in a slightly different direction than you originally anticipated, you have the flexibility to instantly select direct transparencies or change the order accordingly. With slides, preprogrammed computer-generated screens, or to some degree, a predrawn flip chart, you're committed to visual progression decided on before your presentation. Lisa Ford, a very successful speaker who presents full-day customer programs for Career Tracks, uses overheads throughout her program to help her audience stay focused on her points.

The Headaches with Overheads

A problem of overhead projection is the so-called *keystoning effect* you get when you project an image upward on a screen that is typically above the projection area. The image that hits the screen tends to project in the form of the letter V, causing the effect. You can control this by getting the projection equipment as close to the screen as possible and as high up as possible.

Another disadvantage of using an overhead projector versus a flip chart is that, to get a brighter image on the screen, your audience often has to sit in the dark. It also keeps you somewhat in the dark, which is not the best thing for someone who is trying to enlighten an audience. Sometimes, though, you can keep the lights up and still provide a decent view of the screen by having the meeting place personnel remove the light bulbs directly above and in front of the screen.

35 mm Slides

One of the most widely used forms of visuals are 35 mm slides, which are ideally suited to large audiences because slide projectors can produce a large, bold image on the screen. A slide-oriented presentation can be as simple as a single slide projector, which you control, usually by remote control. This remote helps you run a smooth presentation because it takes a minimal amount of effort to advance the next slide. In this way, you can keep your attention focused toward your audience as opposed to constantly turning your back to them to look at the screen.

The main drawback to slides is that you put them in sequence ahead of time and there is no flexibility during your presentation to show them out of that order. You can skip over slides, but that might look unprofessional.

Colorful Impact

Slides are also a medium that can provide you great impact because anything that you can get in a color photograph, artwork or even computer-generated screens can easily be made into slides.

Title slides.   You can use a title slide to stress key points, and you can use a series of progressive title slides that build on key points with one point per line. You do this by starting with a slide with one line for your first point in a high contrasting color. For example, if your background color is a blue, the type might be in bright yellow. The next slide contains the previous line, only in a more muted color like a light blue or pale yellow, and a new line pertaining to your new point in the bright yellow. This process builds.

Like other forms of visual aids, you should keep the content of your slides simple and easy to read. Limit the number of words and element on any given slide. Use easy-to-read type fonts, and make sure that you have a high degree of contrast between the background and the type.

For a more professional look, use a consistent color scheme. This can be further enhanced by using a recurring border that may incorporate your logo or theme. If time and budget permit, consider using a logo, color scheme, and theme of the client's event.

Some speakers who have their slides produced specifically for a client's presentation give the client the slides as an added value when they are done. Sometimes several of the slides are used, with permission, in the client's newsletter when they write an article about your presentation. In the same way, several of the slides could be made available to members of the news media if they attend.

Phil Wexler of La Jolla, California, is a very talented keynoter in the area of customer service and sales. Phil effectively uses professionally produced title slides to reinforce his presentation's key points. Each slide has one very brief reminder of the key point he is making. They are simple and easy to read and reinforce his message, not distract from it.

Illustrative slides.   Slides can be photographs, cartoons, newspaper clips or samples, and examples that you wish to illustrate. Your slides can be produced by a graphic artist or even on your own computer with software programs like *Harvard Graphics.*

Risk management.   You may not want to use slide trays with a higher count than 80 per tray. Especially avoid 120-count trays. The tray is much too tight for the slide to comfortably drop into the machine, possibly causing the slide to jam.

If you have a presentation that requires more than 80 slides and there is no break where you can change trays, you need more than one projector. You could use a dissolve unit, which allows you to have up to three projectors going at once. Many excellent units are available in the marketplace, but the most commonly used for a triple dissolve (three 35 mm slide projectors) is the *Dove X unit.* The Dove X allows you to move from projector A to projector B to projector C, having only one image on the screen at a time. As the image from A dissolves off, the image from B comes in. When you hit the button again, the image from B dissolves out and the image from C comes in. Every time you hit the button on the remote unit or *pickle,* this process repeats.

*T*oasting a *M*aster
DR. MICHAEL LEBOEUF

*M*ichael LeBoeuf, author of *GMP: The Greatest Management Principle in the World* and *How to Win Customers and Keep Them for Life,* uses slides in his speeches based on those two books.

In each speech, he includes a humorous story. In *GMP,* the story involves a frog, a snake, and a man fishing. In *Customers,* the story involves a couple of farmers trying to mate some hogs. In both stories, he uses a "progressive" technique to illustrate the story as he tells it. He had an artist draw the cartoons, which were later turned into the slides, and he shows about seven slides during the entire story.

In the frog story, for example, Dr. LeBoeuf is illustrating his main point that "the actions that get rewarded get done." If you want a certain kind of action or activity done, accomplished, or acted upon, you must reward it. He tells the story of a man who is out in a lake. After some time, he notices over the side of the boat that there is a snake with a frog in its mouth. Feeling sorry for the frog, the fisherman reaches down and gently removes the frog from the snake's mouth. The fisherman then starts to feel sorry for the snake, so he looks for something in the boat to give the snake. He comes up with a half-empty bottle of whisky and gives it to the snake. Pretty soon, the snake swims off happy. Then the frog swims off happy. The fisherman is happy. Everyone is happy. A few minutes later, he hears a knock on the side of the boat. The fisherman looks over and sees the snake, this time with *two* frogs in his mouth!

This technique added to the humor of the story because the cartoon-like illustrations reinforced the verbal presentation. It was also important for keeping the continuity of Dr. LeBoeuf's presentation. Because he uses slides throughout his presentation, the audience may feel uncomfortable not seeing slides during this funny story.

FIGURE 6.2   Sample Slides to Illustrate Story

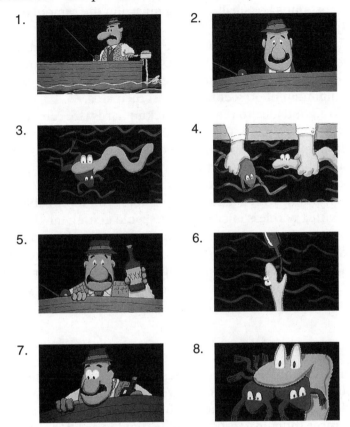

Source: Reprinted by permission of Dr. Michael LeBoeuf.

This allows you to have up to 240 images without changing the slide trays. For presentations that are two hours or less, you may find that two trays are adequate, giving you 160 images during this time period. This dissolve unit makes a much smoother transition between slides than a single projector does.

Many speakers prefer the Kodak dissolve unit because it allows you to advance both forward and backward. On all dissolve units, you can control dissolve rate, which is the period of time it takes the old image to fade out and the new image to fade in.

When using slide projectors, always ask for Bright Light bulbs to give you the brightest image available. Always have a spare bulb for each projector you are using. While wireless equipment is now available for advancing the projectors, you may find that the buttons on most units are small and you must aim the remote directly at the equipment to advance it.

Your alternative is for a "hard-wire" hookup from the projectors and dissolve unit to the area where you're speaking. If you move around on the stage, you should request enough extra wire to move a minimum of 30 feet from the screen area.

It's also a good idea to request a backup hard-wire remote to be laid next to the primary. Occasionally, a short occurs in the wire from someone stepping on the line or good ole Murphy's Law. If there's a problem with your primary remote, you simply pick up the backup remote, and you're back in business.

When working with a hard-wired remote, you'll probably want to work with a wireless microphone to avoid getting tangled up in all the excess wires on the stage. The only wire that is on the stage is the one the remote unit controls. If you have a hard-wire microphone and a hard-wire remote control "pickle" for your projectors, be careful not to move around a lot because you will get tangled up in your own mess.

Visual Extravaganza

Another advantage of using slides is that you can easily keep your visuals current. In some cases, very current. Michael Aun uses a special process where he shoots photographs of people at a convention, turns them instantly into slides, and in as little as an hour later, shows them in his speech.

For almost two decades he has been doing this as part of his programs, and his audiences love it. The main reason, of course, is that *they* are the stars of the show.

The process was patented by Polaroid a number of years ago. The film kit he uses is called PolaChrome 35 mm. Polaroid first introduced the process in a hand-driven developer process, which Michael still uses today. Motor-driven models now exist.

To use this approach, you need a high-quality 35 mm camera, but avoid cameras with built-in flash units as the lighting is absolutely critical to the success of these pictures. When taking pictures of an audience member, try to capture the beauty in their eyes. Shoot close-up, head and shoulder shots, capturing no more than four, and preferably two, people to the shot. Ask them to pose closely, cheek to cheek.

Developing the film takes approximately 60 seconds. You then clip each image, insert it into a mount, and drop it into the tray. The entire process takes less than one hour.

Downside of Slides

The singular biggest disadvantage to using slides over transparencies is the loss of eye contact with your audience. When showing slides, you have to either bring the room lights down or else bury the screen in a darkened corner so that the audience can see the image. Unfortunately, when using slides, many speakers have a tendency to look more at the screen than at their audience.

The other disadvantage to slides is the cost of producing them. If you hire a graphic designer, you could spend a lot of money to produce a slide, but that investment includes the production of the artwork as well as the slide itself, which you can use over and over again. If you have a critical point you're making in a speech, creating that particular slide might be well worth some extra attention.

It is to your advantage to establish contact with a good, dependable source for producing your materials and stick with them. Do not jump around every week to save a nickel here and a dime there. It is not worth the hassle.

Videotape and Computer-Presented Visuals

Fellow NSA member Terry Brock of Atlanta, Georgia, has taken many concepts of using slides into the laptop computer. The very things that many speakers do with slides, he does with his laptop. The production of a graphic image is now more easily accomplished with the laptop and the use of software like *Astound!* In fact, the same software that some audiovisual production companies use to produce slides are being used to produce Terry's video image.

The 35 mm picture that Michael Aun takes with his Nikon camera is being replaced by a live moving image that Terry takes with a video camera. Terry has taken all of Michael's creative concepts and transferred them into the technology that he uses—the computer and the video camera. Everything we have outlined about slides applies to Terry's technology as well, especially the idea about not letting the technology be the speech. You still have to deliver the speech or seminar, and all the video and computer technology in the world cannot take the place of you, the presenter.

Computerized Overheads

The strongest use of this equipment is for teaching people specifics about computer programs. For example, when Jeff and Marc Slutsky give seminars based on their book *Street Smart Tele-Selling: The 33 Secrets* (Prentice-Hall, 1990), they present a module on the use of computerized databases in the telephone selling process. The best way to illustrate the capabilities of a computerized contact manager like *TeleMagic* is to project the computer image directly on screen and take the program through its paces.

But you're not limited to illustrating computer programs on screen. Special software packages like *Astound!* help you computerize your audiovisual presentation. These programs allow you to design screens on your computer with a complete array of text, colors, and illustrations, and you can even incorporate photographic and video images. Then you can sequence the screens any way you wish and even use some limited animation of the text and illustrations.

To present the information, you can use a notebook computer and a projector of which there are two basic types. The first is a piece that lays directly on a standard overhead projector. Though relatively inexpensive, the quality of the screen image is weak and therefore should be limited to use with a relatively small group. For a stronger image for larger groups, you really should use a video projector. This takes the video output directly from your notebook and projects it on screen. These projectors are very expensive, but they provide a relatively crisp image. You can even use these projectors to replace standard monitors for showing videotape.

Most projector units have a remote control that allows you to have the computer go to the next screen just as you do with a slide projector. The big advantage of this feature is that it allows you to keep your eyes on your audience. You don't want to be staring at the screen during your presentation; you should already know what it looks like. It's okay to check to make sure that you have the right screen up and to give yourself a quick reminder of where you are in your presentation, but then look back to your audience.

The Problems with Computerized Visuals

While using this form of audiovisual presentation offers many advantages, you should consider several disadvantages before investing your time and money into it.

Limited availability. Unlike overhead projectors, flip charts, and slide projectors, very few meeting places have video projection equipment. This means that most speakers who use this type of equipment have to buy it and transport it from speech to speech. The other option is that you can find companies that rent this equipment and will ship it to your venue ahead of your presentation, send a courier to pick it up afterward, and insure it for a fee. This is a nice option to have, but its not cheap. Plus you still have to schlep your computer around with you. However, there is some light at the end of the tunnel. This technology is improving all the time. The projection units are becoming smaller and lighter and will likely become increasingly more available in meeting places in the near future.

Limited flexibility. Like 35 mm slides, it is very difficult to change the sequence of your screens while you're in the middle of your presentation. If your audience wants to go in a slightly different direction, you might not be able to bring the visuals along with you.

Limited margin for error. It's very frustrating when visuals aren't working correctly. You increase your chances of technical problems when you combine a computer with a video projector, which is infinitely more complicated than most other forms of visuals. When it works correctly, it is a very impressive presentation, but when it doesn't, you will have what feels like the longest speech of your life.

Limited time.   One other downside to using the presentation software is that you have to either take the time to learn it yourself or you have to hire someone to program it for you. If you plan to make this type of visual a part of your presentation, you really should take the time to master the software. Aside from saving you money in the long run, while you're on the road, you'll want to know how to make changes yourself should something go wrong. And the upside, however, is that once you learn it, you will have the ability to take a standard presentation and customize the visuals with your client's name, logo, and other personal items.

Videotape in Your Presentation

Using videotape during a presentation can have a very dramatic effect on your audience. Jeff Slutsky and his brother Marc use one short video clip to reinforce a key point in their seminar, *Street Fighters: Neighborhood Sales Builders.* This seminar teaches retailers and other local small businesses how to advertise, promote, and market on a community level with only a shoestring budget. One of the segments deals with how to sponsor a fundraiser and turn it into a profit-generating venture for your business while making your business a local hero in the process. They share an example from one of their clients, a Bob's Big Boy.

The general manager of local Bob's Big Boy offered to help raise money for a 12-year-old girl named Valerie, who suffered from cystic fibrosis and desperately needed a double lung transplant to survive. Her family and friends were doing some small fundraising programs and received some local publicity in the Philadelphia media. The manager offered to hold a promotion in which, after accounting for their normal sales, he would donate half of the remainder of all the sales that day.

Valerie's father spearheaded the effort to promote the event with an army of volunteers. The restaurant's general manager arranged for karate demonstrations and an appearance by IBC Super Middleweight Champion Dave Tibers. Door prizes and football tickets were raffled off to help the cause. Even a Big Boy character stood out in the parking lot, waving passing motorists in and drawing attention to the restaurant. The volunteers, some of whom were servers at the restaurant, passed out fliers and put up posters, which were donated by the local quick printer. They handed out announcements door to door and placed them under windshield wipers. They got mentions in the local newspaper and on the radio. The event also was promoted for a week inside the restaurant and on the marquee.

The fundraiser was a huge success—for all parties. This event resulted in the employees and community pulling together for a worthy cause. A total of $2,500 was donated to Valerie and Bob's Big Boy received all the credit. The manager was interviewed on two Philadelphia TV newscasts, and the restaurant received an estimated $20,000 worth of free publicity. Customer counts rose 30 percent, and many of those were new faces.

This program took some *moderate* effort on the part of the manager, but the volunteers did most of the promoting. There was no risk because he donated only money in excess of what the restaurant would normally do on a typical Wednesday. If the group didn't promote the event and sales were flat, there was no donation. When a donation was made, the 50 percent covered the cost of food and labor with the other half going to the cause, which made it a no-risk promotion. Many new customers did visit the store, paying full price for their meals. You could spend twice as much on standard media and not get the type of results that were gained from this type of promotion. And since the restaurant didn't have to use a discount or coupon to motivate those new customers, they had a much better chance of getting them to come back and pay full price.

This fundraiser is a very compelling example of a key point Jeff and Marc try to make in their seminar. But the element that really drives it home is when they play the two Philadelphia newscasts to the audience, after having explained the basics of the event. One screen in the first clip shows a mother of one of Valerie's friends who helped raise some money. The mother breaks down for a moment and cries. When this video clip is finished, the audience at the seminar is greatly impacted.

While presenting to the general assembly at the National Speakers Association annual convention, Dan Jansen, the gold medal ice skating champion from the 1994 Olympics, showed a dramatic 15-minute videotape that was used by ABC Sports. When they showed him winning the gold after all the personal tragedy in his life, there was hardly a dry eye in the place. Though Dan was not a polished speaker, by using videotape in a very dramatic and effective way, he certainly was a memorable one.

Props

Props are generally three-dimensional visual aids that you can use to help reinforce points you're making in your presentation. Props are limited only by your own creativity. (See Chapter 4.) The beauty of Toastmasters International is that you can test your ideas at the local club before taking them into the marketplace. Remember the words on the gridiron at West Point: "On these friendly fields of strife are sown the seeds that on other fields and on other days are borne the fruits of victory." For a speaker, it means that Toastmasters International meetings provide you a low-risk opportunity to work out the bugs of using props in your presentation.

Other words of advice come from the Magnificent Hondo, a speaker who uses magic in his presentations to help his audiences better understand his message. He offers these words: "I now use one piece of magic in my presentations. I do not want to be known as a magician, and it is not likely that anyone will ever confuse me with Hondo, but that single addition to my program was just enough to spice it up and take it to a higher level."

Shep Hyken, in St. Louis, Missouri, is also a master at using magic in his presentations. He even used it for the title of his customer service book entitled *Moments of Magic.*

Michael Aun uses a number of bells, whistles, horns, and other gadgets to make his presentations interesting. People want information delivered in exciting ways. You cannot be afraid to take risks from the platform. The day of the speaker showing up and reading a speech is long behind us.

Sometimes, though, certain props can be downright hazardous. John Patrick Dolan, CPAE, of LawTalk in Brea, California, is a speaker, attorney, and author of *Negotiating Like the Pros.* He uses a pyrotechnic magic trick as a prop in his speech. It's a book that, when opened, briefly shoots out a flame. John uses it to drive home a point in his speech, but it caused him some difficulty when returning from Ireland after speaking there. Security detained him overnight to make sure that this device wasn't a terrorist's bomb.

Larry Winget of Tulsa, Oklahoma, tells a very funny story about the Lone Ranger. He also used a silver bullet as a prop . . . that is, until he got stopped by airport security.

☞ **Master's Tip:** *Go through your speech or seminar outline and identify one point or story where a prop could be used to enhance the message. Make or buy that prop and practice using it in your presentation until you feel comfortable with it. Test it out at your next Toastmasters International meeting and get some feedback. Once you've worked it into your presentation, repeat this process with another prop.*

Chapter 7

*L*eading In with a Perfect Introduction

A bad introduction delivered by an ill-trained introducer can ruin your speech. Conversely, if you receive a great introduction delivered with style and enthusiasm, your speech is likely to get a much better response from the audience. With so much riding on the quality of your introduction, you don't want to risk a slow start to your presentation just because your introducer did a poor job. Also, if you are the introducer, you want to ensure that you give your speaker the momentum needed to launch into an effective presentation.

Introducing You Is an Integral Part of Your Speech

Toastmasters International teaches that every speech has a beginning, a middle, and an end. You should look at your introduction as the very beginning of your beginning. It should not be a totally separate element that is out of your control. You should always prepare and rehearse every part of your speech; you should never just get out there and wing it. Likewise, apply this same effort and intensity to your introduction.

If presented properly, your introduction can help you launch into your speech with great momentum. A good introduction is like an aircraft carrier catapult that gives jet fighters their initial boost on their journey. Furthermore, since someone else gives your introduction, you can more easily have them "toot your horn" whereas it might appear arrogant or egotistical for you, yourself, to mention certain elements about your talents.

Goals of a Successful Introduction

Your introduction can help launch your speech and set the mood and pace. Below are three primary goals of your introduction:

1. *Establish your credibility.* Once the audience has heard your introduction, they should have no doubt that you bring the necessary credentials, experience, and knowledge to address your subject.
2. *Establish your intent.* After hearing your introduction, the audience knows the reason for your speech and how you expect them to benefit from taking their time to hear it. In short, it helps "sell" the audience on why they need to pay attention to your presentation.
3. *Establish your background.* The audience learns, through your introduction, a little of how you got your credibility.

Elements of a Successful Introduction

An introduction consists of two elements: the *message* and the *messenger.* Between the two, you have much greater control over the message, yet you can use several tactics to help any messenger present your introduction better.

The message and the messenger must work together. You can reduce the risk of getting a weak introduction by controlling as much of the introduction as possible. Here are some suggestions:

Always provide a written introduction.   Never leave the text of your introduction up to anyone else. Always provide it written the way you want it read. Also, make your introduction easy to read. Use 14 point type and provide on the page only what you want read. Don't put instructions in parentheses if possible, because there is a good chance someone will read them aloud. Think of the impression the audience has after hearing an introducer read, "He is the author of three books. (Show book now)." It makes both you and the introducer look bad.

Review your written introduction with your introducer. Provide your introducer with a copy of your written introduction well ahead of the program. Also, when sending an advance copy of the introduction, include a cover letter that makes it clear to your introducer that you want the introduction read exactly as provided. Be sure to include a reason for your request so you don't come off like a *prima donna*. One reason might be that you find that this gives you the best audience response. Be careful though, it's not uncommon for an introducer to start by saying, "I'm now going to introduce our speaker with this introduction he gave me." That preamble costs credibility.

Once at the meeting place, be sure to review one more time what you want your introducer to do. You may want to point out several spots in the introduction that have caused others a little difficulty, like the correct pronunciation of your name. If your introducer wants to make changes, make sure that you first approve them.

Make sure that your introducer finishes all "housekeeping" details first. If your introducer has to make announcements that are unrelated to your presentation, suggest that this be done before starting your introduction. Some inexperienced introducers will read the speaker's introduction then say, "Before we bring our speaker out, I have a few announcements." Then when you do start your speech, the audience forgets what they learned from your introduction, and you lose the momentum from a well-written, well-presented, and well-timed intro.

These same suggestions apply to the end of your presentation. You want to leave your audience on a "high note." If there is housekeeping to do at the end, suggest that they do it before your introduction so that you are the last thing the audience remembers.

Writing Your Introduction

The first step in preparing your introduction is to identify all those experiences, credentials, and accomplishments that you feel would help your audience understand the reason you're qualified to give this presentation. Here are some suggestions to get you started:

☞ **Master's Tips**

1. ***Do a thorough inventory*** *of all your strengths and weaknesses, simply listing them in any particular order.*

2. ***List all your accomplishments and honors.*** *Prepare your personal resume. Be as generous as you did when you applied for that first job (you remember when you searched your brain for every honor). Again, do not list them in any particular order.*

3. ***List all the reasons*** *why any particular audience would want to hear from you. What makes you an expert on the topic, and why?*

4. ***List all professional designations and educational achievements,*** *again in no order of preference.*

5. ***List whatever personal facts about your background you feel are relevant.*** *Michael Aun happens to use his family as examples in all his presentations. Jeff Slutsky always mentions that he owned several small businesses and the marketing dollars came out of his own pockets. Include this kind of information only if it is relevant to your presentation.*

6. ***List the media attention you have received as well as your publishing accomplishments,*** *including writing or contributing to books, audiocassette programs, video or television programs, radio programs, interactive software programs, manuals, and articles. If you've written more than two books, for example, you may want to condense your list. For example, Jeff's introduction says, "He's the author of six books, including* Street Fighting *and* How to Get Clients.*" The two books he mentions of the six are the ones that he feels give him the most credibility with this audience. If Jeff or Michael are speaking to a group of speakers, one of the two books they would men-*

tion in their introduction would be The Toastmasters International® Guide to Successful Speaking.

7. **List extracurricular activities,** *including nonprofit organizations and charities in any particular order.*

8. **List your contributions** *in any area related to the group you are addressing.*

9. **Decide how much personal information you want to share** *about your spouse, children, extended family, and so on.*

10. *Once you have gathered these facts,* **review your list** *and sort the items into three categories:*
    a. *must mention in every introduction;*
    b. *could mention if time allowed;*
    c. *should mention only to a particular group.*

11. **When writing your basic, general introduction, include only items from an "A" category list.**

12. *When writing customized introductions for specific clients,* **include appropriate items** *from all three categories.*

13. **Keep it short.** *Try to limit your introduction to three paragraphs.*

Outlining Your Introduction

The beginning. Like a speech, a good introduction has a beginning, a middle, and an end. The beginning of an introduction is much like the headline of an advertisement. It should sell the benefit of the program. You want to capture the interest of your audience immediately.

The middle. The middle of your introduction contains the credibility elements. These are the accomplishments and recognitions that give you the right to present this information.

The end. You want to get your audience mentally prepared for the presentation at the end of the introduction. This is also where you give a call to action to the audience to receive the speaker. Often this would be something like, "Please help me welcome . . ." or "Let's give a warm (*name of the group*) welcome

to . . ." This tells the audience to applaud, which sets a more re-
ceptive tone.

Sample Introductions

To see how these different elements would fit together, look at
Jeff Slutsky and Michael Aun's standard introductions:

> **Jeff Slutsky intro.** Our speaker today entitles his presenta-
> tion, "Confessions of a Street Fighter," and shares with us some
> of his streetwise secrets on how we can outthink our
> competition . . . not outspend them.
>
> With a background in both advertising and public relations,
> Jeff Slutsky had an opportunity to practice what he preached
> when he became part owner of a nightclub and later a health
> club. With the marketing dollars now coming out of his *own*
> pocket, he soon began to discover and develop result-oriented,
> low-cost tactics to build sales. This unique combination of
> shrewd thinking, innovative problem solving, budgeting on a
> shoestring, and a lot of hard work, came to be known as *street
> fighting.*
>
> Jeff is the founder and president of Street Fighter® Marketing
> in Columbus, Ohio, and he is the author of six books, including
> *Street Fighting,* which is part of the *Street Fighter's Profit Pack-
> age,* a complete video- and audio-training program with tele-
> phone consulting.
>
> His Street Fighting program has received a great deal of na-
> tional media attention, including *The Wall Street Journal, USA
> Today, Success, Inc.* magazine, CNN, and *Sally Jessy Raphael,*
> and Jeff is a regular on the PBS series *Small Business Today.*
> Jeff's street fighting client list includes AT&T, McDonald's,
> American Express, Walt Disney, Pizza Hut, Honda, Sony, Good-
> year, Marvel Comics, the city of Dallas, the state of Arkansas,
> and the country of India.
>
> Please help me welcome a real street fighter, Jeff Slutsky.
>
> **Michael Aun's intro.** Our speaker today is a man of varying
> background. As a successful businessperson, he has presided
> over a real estate development firm, a construction business, a
> nationally acclaimed family-owned restaurant, and a successful
> insurance practice.

As a writer, his popular column, "Behind the Mike" has been syndicated for over 25 years and has appeared in 60 different newspapers and periodicals. He has coauthored four books, including his first, *Build a Better You, Starting Now,* part of a 26-volume series. His section entitled "Get Up, You're Killing The Grass!," has been widely acclaimed. Royal Publishing produced his second and third books, *The Great Communicators* and *Marketing Masters,* and Dearborn his fourth, *The Toastmasters International Guide to Successful Speaking.* Our speaker has produced a dozen audio-learning systems, two dozen video-training modules, and he has written over 300 articles and booklets on sales, management, leadership, customer service, change, relationship strategies, communication, motivation, and inspiration.

Our speaker rose to international acclaim in 1978 when he won the World Championship of Public Speaking for Toastmasters International in Vancouver, British Columbia. He won the coveted honor by defeating eight other speakers representing some 150,000 Toastmasters from the 55-country Toastmasters International Speaking World. He has since delivered over 2,000 presentations and has shared the lectern with Presidents Carter, Reagan and Bush, as well as a host of celebrities including such speaking giants as Paul Harvey, Dr. Norman Vincent Peale, Kenneth McFarland, Art Linkletter, Zig Ziglar, Tom Peters, Mark Russell, and others.

In 1983, our speaker was presented the prestigious Certified Speaking Professional designation by the National Speakers Association (NSA) and was one of the fewer than 150 speakers in the world to be so honored at that time. In 1989, the 3,500-member NSA body elected him to their Board of Directors.

Ladies and gentlemen, let's welcome from Kissimmee, Florida, . . . Michael Aun!

You'll probably notice some similarities in these two introductions although they are geared for different types of audiences. In both cases, these introductions give the speakers' key credentials, accomplishments, and credibility, which let the audience know the speakers are qualified to deliver the presentation.

*T*oasting a *M*aster
PATRICIA FRIPP

*P*atricia Fripp is a wonderfully talented speaker who is also a master at giving introductions. Patricia's secret for giving super introductions is that she treats the introduction with the same seriousness as giving a speech. Ideally, she wants to memorize the introductions she gives, or if she needs to use notes, she uses one-word cues to remind her of critical key points. Another important point to giving great introductions is to keep them short. As an introducer, you are not the focal point. The speaker is. Don't upstage your speaker.

Patricia usually gets a standard introduction or biographical material, but then she gives it her own twist geared toward the circumstances. For example, she introduced Rosita Perez, one of the most popular speakers at the NSA annual convention. Most of the audience knew both Rosita and Patricia. Both have spoken to this group many times. So Patricia's challenge was to not only set up Rosita's credibility but also to share some new information about her. She used humor in that introduction by exaggerating points. Rosita always wears flowers in her hair. Patricia always wears flamboyant hats. For Rosita's introduction, Patricia wore a big rimmed hat with flowers and used it for an interesting comparison in the introduction.

By contrast, Patricia introduced Art Berg, CPAE, to an NSA convention audience with an entirely different approach. Art is a quadriplegic who is a very funny motivational speaker but was virtually unknown to this audience. Art's presentation followed a very emotional presentation about the organization's involvement in "Give the Kids the World," which provides special services for terminally ill children. Patricia used very short sentences and told the audience all of Art's accomplishments, including participating in a super marathon. She played it straight because she wanted to change the energy for Art. His presentation was unforgettable and was perfectly set up by Patricia's introduction.

☞ More Master's Tips:

- *Read your introduction onto an audiocassette tape and time it.* Try to limit the time to 60 seconds unless you have something very special to share.

- *Sound it out.* If your own voice introducing you sounds "iffy," chances are that someone else reading it is not going to sound much better. Avoid tongue twisters; make the copy pleasant to hear. For example, Jeff often listed three books in his introduction that would normally not be a problem. But the one he listed were Street Fighting, Street Smart Marketing, *and* Street Smart Tele-Selling. *Try saying that three times fast. As it turned out, most introducers can't even say it one time slow!* So he now uses two books and at least one without the word "Street" in it. Another area of his introduction that gave some introducers problems was when he listed the national media attention he received. One publication that featured his program was Inc. *magazine. Some people would spell it out, "I, N, C, magazine." So in the introduction, he wrote it as "*Ink *magazine." It sounded right, but many would stop their introduction to mention the "typo." Finally, he would go over the introduction with them and just point it out so there would be no confusion.*

- *Consider using humor in your introduction,* especially if your nature is to use lots of humor in your speech. One little chuckle that Jeff gets in his introduction is at the end of his list of clients. It goes like this, "Jeff's street fighting client list includes AT&T, McDonald's, American Express, Walt Disney, Pizza Hut, Honda, Sony, Goodyear, Marvel Comics, the city of Dallas, the state of Arkansas, and the country of India." The "country of India" usually gets them, provided the introducer doesn't call it the country of Indiana or the county of India, which has happened several times.

- *Always print your introduction on plain white paper,* and use type no smaller than 14 points.

- *Do not print thousands of copies of your intro.* You will want to update it with every appropriate new event that occurs in your life.

- *Tailor your introductions with as much personal information about the group as possible.*

- *Interview your Master of Ceremonies in advance to learn as much about them and their group as possible.*
- **Know who the backup Master of Ceremonies will be.**

Bad Introduction Horror Story

It was a cold, miserable evening in Boise, Idaho. Michael Aun was speaking to 100 of the townspeople who had braved sub-freezing weather, snow, and ice to come to hear him address the monthly club meeting. Michael had prepared his normal one-minute introduction and had it ready for the Master of Ceremonies to read word for word. When the emcee took the podium, Michael saw him grasping what appeared to be some 15 pages of paper. He was struck with horror. Michael realized that the one-minute biographical sketch was replaced by what had to be a thorough credit report. This guy had information about Michael that even he had forgotten. He even knew the names of his kids and his dogs. The obviously had made a prodigious effort to know Michael inside and out, and he was determined to tell the loyal folks in Boise everything he knew and more.

Twenty-eight minutes later, Michael took the platform. What should have been a very simple process for the person introducing Michael turned from "15 minutes of fame" into "28 minutes of folly" for the Master of Ceremonies and a horror story for Michael as the speaker.

By the time Michael finally spoke his first word, nearly 75 percent of the audience members had departed for parts unknown. Those who remained did so out of courtesy. However, the damage had been done. Nothing Michael could do could salvage the evening, but he learned a valuable lesson: Never again let an introduction go beyond 60 seconds.

This was actually the second occasion during which this sort of thing happened to Michael. When he was 21 years old, he was elected Grand Knight of Bishop England Council 724 of the Knights of Columbus in Columbia, South Carolina, a remarkable event unto itself since the average age of the membership of that council was in the late 60s.

The Knights were very fortunate to have accomplished quite a few notable achievements during his tenure as Grand Knight, including the completion of a 16-story highrise for the moderate-income elderly known as Christopher Towers. As a result, the Supreme Knight of the Knights of Columbus, John McDevitt, honored them by visiting Columbia, South Carolina, to be their keynote speaker at their June Ball and Awards Banquet.

Since the demand on his time was tremendous, it was next to impossible for a small Knights of Columbus Council in the deep South to be able to secure a speaker of Mr. McDevitt's caliber and stature. He had already turned down speaking engagements for not only the South Carolina State Council but state councils in every neighboring state. However, he agreed to come to their little awards dinner.

They selected the most eloquent spokesperson in the South Carolina State Council of the Knights of Columbus to introduce the Supreme Knight. The Supreme Knight had sent down some seven pages of biographical data, some of which should have been selected to properly introduce him.

Thirty-four minutes after he began the introduction, the Master of Ceremonies finally took his seat. The Supreme Knight McDevitt was livid. He stood at the podium, reached into his right coat pocket, and took out a note from his wife. "The note," he related, "was four simple letters . . . K – I – S – S! I asked my wife what it meant," he went on, "and she said to <u>Keep</u> <u>It</u> <u>Short</u> and <u>Sweet</u>. I wish I had told the Master of Ceremonies that!" he added.

The Prerecorded, Preproduced Introduction

One way to avoid the risk of getting a bad introduction is to do your own. Many speakers rarely speak in any format today where they're not using some form of audiovisual support, either videotape or 35 mm slides. Since the equipment needed for this kind of introduction is the same equipment used in the regular presentation, you may choose never to be a victim of another 28-minute introduction. If you suspect that the introducer is not going to bring you on like you want the person to, push for the "electronic high-tech" option.

Michael's friend and NSA colleague, Al McCree, helped produce his introductory audiotape for him. They hired a good Nashville voice-over to read the script, which was kept very brief and to the point, and most importantly under a minute in length. Al then synchronized the voice-over to music—and bingo!—they have a wonderful audiotape that they can use anywhere.

Next, Michael gathered his collection of pictures and slides that reinforced the spoken message in the introduction. When the voice-over mentions that Michael is a Life and Qualifying Member of the Million Dollar Round Table and that he has spoken to that body's Main Platform, slides of this appear on the screen.

Michael picked up this idea from his friend and mentor, the late Jim Valvano, who led the North Carolina State Wolfpack basketball team to a National Championship. "Jimmy V," as they called him, had a video segment of him running across the floor after winning the NCAA National Title with a wonderful voice-over and music. Michael thought that this was a terrific introduction, but he himself had not won any national basketball championships.

However, he had won a world championship, the World Championship of Public Speaking for Toastmasters International. And not only that, he had written books and produced tapes and training programs. He had a syndicated column for over 25 years. He had built businesses. He had shared the lectern with presidents and celebrities. In fact, he had many such things that he could say and reinforce with visual aids. Why not use them?

The biggest challenge in putting this together was not to get egotistical in preparing the script and the information being conveyed. Part of you says that you need to say some of these things to give you credibility. Part of you says that you need humility. Both parts are right, and both should be measured and used in moderation.

When Michael uses the electronic introduction, it does not negate the need for a Master of Ceremonies. Someone has to introduce the introduction, but what they say is kept to a minimum. In huge, bold 25 point type, the script for the introducer says:

> "Ladies and gentlemen,
> we have produced a very special
> high-tech introduction of our
> keynote speaker. So sit back,
> relax, and enjoy as we introduce
> Michael Aun!"

At that point, the lights in the room are dimmed, and the recorded introduction with musical background fills the chamber as images hit the screen in rapid-fire fashion, either in the form or slides or a video of the same format.

During the next 60 seconds, some 140 images appear, some staying up for only a fraction of a second. The visual images reinforce the spoken word and say more about the speaker than the copy ever could.

The quickest way for you to lose credibility as a speaker is to address a topic on which you know little. You must "walk the walk to talk the talk," as we affectionately say at our NSA conferences. Audiences will no longer tolerate the same old worn-out stories and humor. As noted previously, they want information delivered *"with CNN timing and MTV pizazz,"* especially if they are paying top dollar to hear you speak.

Focusing on Your Audience

Your introduction must focus on what is important to your audience. For instance, when Michael speaks to teachers, he always mentions that he is a father of three sons and was involved as their Scoutmaster, coach, and Sunday school teacher. Those credentials would mean very little to AT&T or NASA audiences, but they might have much more credibility for his audience of teachers than the fact that he won some world championship of public speaking.

When he speaks to salespeople, they want to know what he has sold and whether he was successful. Why should they spend their money and time listening to some guy who has never sold anything? When he speaks to managers, they want to know if he knows something about managing people. Michael has recruited, trained, and motivated a sales force for most of his adult life. That gives him the credibility he needs when he talks about managing others. Your life is not a dress rehearsal. It is the real thing, and what you have done in your life is what gives you credibility on the platform.

When Michael speaks to audiences on leadership, they want to know what risks he's taken in his own life. Where has he succeeded and failed? How did he deal with those setbacks? For example, Michael ran for the House of Representatives when he lived in South Carolina in 1980 and lost, big time. Ironically, speaking about his defeat probably means more to his audiences than if he had won.

Everything you do in your life screams volumes about you, and you must focus on why you are special to this audience. Make sure that your introductions fit the group to whom you are speaking. If you speak regularly in a certain industry, you should have a specialized introduction just for that industry. You may want to include such things as offices you've held in your trade association, articles you've written for your trade journals, articles written about you, the companies in your industry that you've worked with or for, and perhaps some good quotes from respected leaders in your industry.

For example, Michael's insurance industry introduction mentions many professional designations that he has earned in that industry as well as the major honors accorded his agency and himself for sales or management performance. It's likely that the good folks at IBM could care less that he has an FIC (Fraternal Insurance Counselor) designation or an LUTCF (Life Underwriter Training Council Fellow) designation or that he is a Life and Qualifying Member of the Million Dollar Round Table.

When Jeff Slutsky speaks to restaurant groups, he modifies his introduction so that the list of clients might include McDonald's, Pizza Hut, Subway, Baskin-Robbins, Dairy Queen, Domino's Pizza, Bob's Big Boy, TGI Friday's, The National Restaurant Association, Multiple Food Service Operators, etc. The paragraph listing the media attention he has received might then include *Nation's Restaurant News, Restaurants and Institutions, Pizza Today,* etc. When speaking to automotive aftermarket groups, he would change that paragraph to include Goodyear, Honda, Firestone, Minit Lube, Ziebart, Chevron, etc.

Also, failing to mention your books and tapes on any topic that will reinforce your credibility in those particular areas of expertise is just plain negligence on your part. These are the very facts that will appeal most to that particular audience.

Chapter 8

*P*reparing the Inspirational/Motivational Keynote Address

*T*here will always be a place for motivational material in almost every kind of presentation. Our audiences are looking to us for inspiration and leadership. The spoken word is an ideal medium for delivering a motivational or inspirational message.

Toastmasters International values this topic so much that the organization devotes one of its ten major projects to the subject, "Inspire Your Audience." The uplifting and inspirational talk challenges people to embrace noble motives or achieve their highest potential. Like Toastmasters International, the National Speakers Association (NSA) also places much significance on topics of motivation and inspiration. NSA offers its members access to a Motivational Keynote Professional Emphasis Group [PEG], which provides special sessions on helping speakers better succeed in this arena.

Inspiration Versus Motivation

Most people use the terms *inspiration* and *motivation* interchangeably. But according to Larry Winget, a top motivational speaker, the inspirational speech merely makes the audience feel good, whereas the motivational speech does that plus asks the audience to take action. Larry feels that all speeches should be motivational. Even if you are giving a somewhat technical presentation, the goal of your speech should be to have your audience make a change or do something after hearing you speak. Inspiration, Larry feels, is just one tool that a motivational speech uses to set up the call to action.

Realities about Motivation

Many people mistakenly feel that listening to a motivational speech can make a big difference in their lives. It is possible, but the realities are that, in most situations, you'll discover some limits to what you can accomplish through a motivational speech. Some of these realities include the following:

1. *Everyone is motivated.* Motivation can be positive or negative. Even a person who decides to stay in bed instead of going to work is motivated. Though the motivation is negative, it is nonetheless a motivation.

2. *You cannot expect to motivate anyone to do anything they do not want to do.* Motivation is an internal issue, not an external one.

3. *People act for their reasons, not for yours.* Since you cannot motivate people to do anything they do not want to do, then the best you can do as a motivational keynote speaker is provide them with an environment where the audience members are encouraged to act with your message.

4. *You have unique and special responsibilities.* Even though you cannot motivate people to do anything they do not want to do, be careful of what you are trying to motivate them to do. The motivational speech, presented properly, is extremely powerful. It can be a catalyst to start and end wars. Do everything in *your* power to make sure that your call to action is fair and appropriate. A good speaker with a bad message is trouble. Remember, Adolf Hitler was a very powerful motivational speaker; however, his call to action was very evil.

*T*oasting a *M*aster
W. MITCHELL, CSP, CPAE

W. Mitchell is a master motivational speaker. First, his very appearance establishes his credibility. He rolls himself onto the stage in a wheelchair. He slowly pans his audience with his fire-scarred face. Then with a slight smile, he says, "Have you ever been in prison? I have. I'm a prisoner to this wheelchair." He then goes on to explain that while riding his motorcycle home one afternoon, a delivery truck hit him. At this point, he didn't need a wheelchair yet. However, the fire that resulted from the impact burned him beyond recognition, causing him to lose all his fingers and seriously burning over 75 percent of his body.

He tells of his remarkable recovery and how he went on to build a major company that had over 2,000 employees. Mitchell was even elected mayor of a small Colorado town and helped save a mountain from destruction by developers. As if that were not enough, Mitchell then relates the second half of his tragic story of how he was flying a small airplane one day and the equipment simply quit on him, causing the plane to crash. Again he survived, but he suffered major injuries and was destined to be confined to a wheelchair for the rest of his life. Most of us would have given up after either of these remarkable events but not Mitchell.

The stories are very dramatic, yet most of his speech revolves around his theme of "It's not what happens to you, it's what you do about it." He doesn't dwell on the tragedies but on the triumphs. And when he's done, he leaves you with a call to action to do something positive in your life and not to use the tragedies as your excuse for failure.

Developing Your Motivational Speech

Establishing Your Style

A motivational speech can have many different styles. The style you choose depends on your objective for giving the speech, the audiences' objectives in hearing the speech, and your own personal experiences. Some more common styles of motivational speeches seem to fall into four different categories: the hero, the survivor, the religious, and the success. These four categories may overlap with each other, and it is possible that your motivational speech falls into several categories at the same time.

The hero.   Sports figures, political figures, and military personalities generally use this style. They tell the story of how they achieved their success and offer some private insights to add a unique twist. When General Norman Schwartzkopf or basketball superstar Michael Jordan gives a motivational speech, the audience expects to hear how they succeeded. The hero has credibility by virtue of his or her celebrity status. The actual presentation often is secondary to the person making the presentation.

The survivor.   Professional motivational speakers use this style to share their story about a tragedy or adversity that they overcame. Learning of the speaker's misfortune causes the audience to empathize with the speaker. Then once the audience learns how the speaker lived past that event, the audience member begins to apply those survival principles in his or her own situation that, by comparison to the speaker's, is an easy move. Most professional motivational speakers are not household names, but two of the best are W. Mitchell and Larry Winget, who are toasted in this chapter.

The religious.   The religious-oriented motivational speaker uses quotes from the Bible and other religious publications or personalities to stress the key points. Do not confuse a religious motivational speech with those motivational speakers who refer to religion and God in their presentations. Some motivational speakers may use their faith as one of several means of dealing with their tragedy. However, the goal of a religious motivational speech is to motivate the audience to take action specifically dealing with their relationship with God and according to the doctrine prescribed by that particular denomination. Ministers like Dr. Robert Schuller and Pat Robertson are examples of religious motivational speakers.

The success.   Often used by business executives who tell how they achieved their success in business, this speaker offers several points on how the audience members can achieve their success. In structure, this is similar to the hero and to a degree also depends on the speaker's fame to help carry his or her message. Examples of this type of motivational speaker include Harvey McKay and Lee Iacocca.

Establishing Your Credibility

The first thing you have to do as a motivational keynote speaker is to answer the audience's question, "What gives you the right to present your message?" One key element of a good motivational speech is some kind of self-disclosure. What personal experience have you had that has put you in the position you are now in? The hero and the success gain their credibility through their accomplishments. The religious speaker gains credibility through the knowledge of religion and recognition in that area. The survivor establishes credibility by dealing with some kind of adversity, perhaps even a personal tragedy that was overcome.

Toasting Another Master
LARRY WINGET

*L*arry Winget is another successful professional motivational speaker who uses a completely different style from Mitchell. Larry, like Mitchell, is a survivor; he built a successful business, then lost everything. In his presentation, Larry uses wall-to-wall humor. Here is an excerpt called "The Cowboy" from his motivational speech. This same story appears in Larry's book, *The Simple Way to Success* and also appears in *The New York Times* bestseller, *A 2nd Helping of Chicken Soup for the Soul* by Jack Canfield and Mark Hansen:

> When I started my telecommunications company, I knew I was going to need salespeople to help me expand the business. I put the word out that I was looking for qualified salespeople and began the interviewing process. The salesperson I had in

mind was experienced in the telecommunications industry; knew the local market; had experience with the various types of systems available; had a professional demeanor; and was a self-starter. I had very little time to train a person, so the salesperson I hired had to be able to "hit the ground running."

During the tiresome process of interviewing prospective salespeople, into my office walked a cowboy. I knew he was a cowboy by the way he was dressed. He had on corduroy pants and a corduroy jacket that didn't match the pants; a tie which came about half-way down his chest with a knot bigger than my fist; cowboy boots; and a baseball cap. You can imagine what I was thinking: "Not what I had in mind for my new company." He sat down in front of my desk, took off his cap and said, "Mister, I'd just shore appreciate a chance to be a success in the telephone biness." And that's just how he said it, too: *biness.*

I was trying to figure out a way to tell this fellow without being too blunt that he just wasn't what I had in mind at all.

I asked him about his background. He said he had a degree in agriculture from Oklahoma State University and that he had been a ranch hand in Bartlesville, Oklahoma, for the past few years during the summers. He announced that was all over now, he was ready to be a success in "biness," and he would just "shore appreciate a chance."

We continued to talk, and he was so focused on success and how he would "shore appreciate a chance" that I decided to give him a chance. I told him that I would spend two days with him. In those two days I would teach him everything I thought he needed to know to sell one type of a very small telephone system. At the end of those two days he would be on his own. He asked me how much money I thought he could make.

I told him, "Looking like you look, and knowing what you know, the best you can do is about $1,000 per month." I went on to explain that the average commission on the small telephone systems he would be selling was approximately $250 per system. I told him if he would see one hundred prospects per month, that he would sell four of those prospects a telephone system. Selling four telephone systems would give him a thousand dollars. I hired him on straight commission, with no base salary.

He said that sounded great to him because the most he had ever made was $400 per month as a ranch hand and he was ready to make some money. The next morning, I sat him down to cram as much of the telephone "biness" I could into a 22-year-old cowboy with no business experience, no telephone experience, and no sales experience. He looked like anything but a professional salesperson in the telecommunications business. In fact, he had none of the qualities I was looking for in an employee, except one: He had an incredible focus on being a success.

At the end of two days of training, Cowboy (that's what I called him then, and still do) went to his cubicle. He took out a sheet of paper and wrote down four things:

1. I will be a success in business.
2. I will see 100 people per month.
3. I will sell four telephone systems per month.
4. I will make $1,000 per month.

He placed this sheet of paper on the cubicle wall in front of him and started to work. At the end of the first month he hadn't sold four telephone systems. However, at the end of his first ten days, he had sold seven systems. At the end of his first year, Cowboy hadn't earned $12,000 in commissions. Instead, he had earned over $60,000 in commissions.

He was indeed amazing. One day, he walked into my office with a contract and payment on a telephone system. I asked him how he had sold this one. He said, "I just told her, 'Ma'am, if it don't do nothing but ring and you answer it, it's a heck of a lot prettier than that one you got.'" She bought it.

The lady wrote him a check in full for the telephone system, but Cowboy wasn't really sure I would take a check so he drove her to the bank and had her get cash to pay for the system. He carried a handful of thousand dollar bills into my office and said, "Larry, did I do good?" I assured him that he did good!

After three years, he owned half of my company. At the end of another year, he owned three other companies. At the time we separated as business partners, he was driving a $32,000 black pickup truck. He was wearing $600 cowboy cut suits, $500 cowboy boots, and a three-carat horseshoe-shaped diamond ring. He had become a success in "biness."

What made Cowboy a success? Was it because he was a hard worker? That helped. Was it because he was smarter than everyone else? No. He knew nothing about the telephone business when he started. So what was it? I believe it was because he knew *The Simple Way To Success.*

He was focused on success. He knew that's what he wanted and he went after it.

He took responsibility. He took responsibility for where he was, who he was, and what he was (a ranch hand). Then he took *action* to make it different.

He made a decision to leave that ranch in Bartlesville, Oklahoma, and to look for opportunities to become a success.

He changed. There was no way that he could keep doing the things that he had been doing and receive different results. And he was *willing* to do what was necessary to make success happen for him.

He had a vision and goals. He saw himself as a success. He also had written down specific goals. He wrote down the four items that he intended to accomplish and put them on the wall in front of him. He saw those goals every day and focused on their accomplishment.

He put action to his goals and stayed with it even when it got tough. It wasn't always easy for him. He experienced slumps like everyone else does. He got doors slammed in his face and telephones in his ear more than any other salesperson I have ever known. But he never let it stop him. He kept on going.

He asked. Boy, did he ask! First, he asked me for a chance, then he asked nearly everyone he came across if they wanted to buy a telephone system from him. And his asking paid off. As he likes to put it, "Even a blind hog finds an acorn every once in a while." That simply means that if you ask enough, eventually someone will say yes.

He cared. He cared about me and about his customers. He discovered that when he cared more about taking care of his customers than he cared about taking care of himself, it wasn't long before he didn't have to worry about taking care of himself.

Most of all, **Cowboy started every day as a winner!** He hit the front door expecting something good to happen. He believed that things were going to go his way regardless of what happened. He had no expectation of failure, only an expectation of success. And I've found that when you expect success and take action on that expedition, you almost always get success.

Cowboy has made millions of dollars. He has also lost it all, only to get it back again. In his life, as in mine, it has been proven that once you know and practice the principles of success, they will work for you again and again.

Cowboy is an example to all of us. He especially inspires and encourages me because I have the privilege of knowing him and seeing him exhibit the courage it takes to win. He can also be an inspiration to you. He is proof that it's not environment, or education, or technical skills and ability that make you a success. He proves that it takes more: It takes the principles we so often overlook or take for granted. These are the principles of *"The Simple Way to Success."*

The Simple Way to Success. Self-published by Larry Winget, Win Seminars (800-749-4597). Reprinted with permission.

Building Your Motivational Message

With your credibility established through your experience, you earn the right to tell your story. But now you have to engage your audience by presenting this message in a compelling and entertaining way. Humor and drama are the two most common techniques used by motivational speakers to engage their audience. Most motivational speakers will use elements of both humor and drama in their speech, but usually they weight their presentations one way or another.

Borrowing Adversity When None Exists within You

If you have no dramatic personal adversity to share with your audience, you might then have to share the experience of another to make your point. Commonly used figures include Babe Ruth and Abraham Lincoln, so be unique and find a role model that no one else is using. If your role model is alive, see if you can interview the person you want to use in your motivational story. Get their permission to share their message and make sure that you credit them accordingly. In one of Michael Aun's motivational speeches, he shares a story about the late, great Olympic runner Wilma Rudolph. He interviewed Wilma to learn more about the tremendous obstacles she overcame in her life. She has been a tremendous inspiration to others. Michael still uses that story to illustrate an example of commitment. Here is her story as Michael likes to tell it. The story comes in the middle of his presentation on the heels of comments he is making about commitment.

The Miracle of Wilma Rudolph

When I think of commitment, I think of a story about a young handicapped black child by the name of Wilma Rudolph. She was born premature, weighing four and one-half pounds, on a farm in the backwoods of Tennessee. At the age of four, she was stricken with double pneumonia and scarlet fever. The deadly combination left her with a paralyzed and useless left leg. Doctors told her mother that Wilma would never walk, at least not like a normal child. Her mother's only response was a line from a favorite hymn. Wilma could "climb her highest mountain if she only did it one step at a time."

The first step was very painful. Wilma's doctors had to teach her to walk with a burdensome steel brace. That took five torturous years. At first, walking was impossible, but Wilma's mother continued to massage the impaired leg until one day she achieved a slight step.

The difficult and painful process continued, sustained by the patient dedication of Wilma's mother, who ingrained in her daughter's mind the words, "Never give up!"

On her ninth birthday, Wilma amazed her doctors by taking a step without the steel brace. She had spent the past five years developing her broken, limping step into a smooth, rhythmic stride. Doctors hoped that she would eventually walk without a limp. But what happened in Wilma Rudolph's life amazed the medical world but not her mom.

When she was 13 years old, three things happened to Wilma. First, she entered a Tennessee high school. Second, she joined the track team. And third, she assumed the nickname "limpy Rudolph" because she limped into last place in every event in which she competed.

At first, her friends encouraged her, but when it became apparent to them that she would never compete effectively and that she was suffering abuse from teammates and opponents alike, they urged her—even begged her—to quit.

Wilma continued to enter every race and continued to limp into last place each time, but she always finished. She never quit. One day, a miracle happened. She surprised her teammates by coming in next to last in a race. Another day she finished third from last. One day she finished second from first, and one day she won a race!

Now, with a feeling of victory in her blood, she began to run with a reckless abandon until one day she won every race she entered. That day, she won herself a new nickname, "lightning Rudolph!"

This unknown athlete came to the attention of Coach Ed Temple at Tennessee State University, and he was impressed. Coach Temple asked Wilma to come to his school and run for him. Wilma said, "If running will get me an education, Coach, I will come to your school, and I will run harder and faster than I have ever run in my entire life. I promise you . . . I'll never give up!"

While away at school, things were about to change again for Wilma. No longer could she depend on the motivation of her mother. Motivation had to come from within.

Wilma was brilliant in her college career. In 1960, both she and her coach received the honor of being picked for the Olympic track team that was to compete in Rome.

Wilma had never traveled outside Tennessee, except to compete with the track team. A dramatic stage had been set for this poor black child who had fought her way out of the shackles of a leg brace to compete in the Olympics.

Those in the stadium that year in Rome thought that Wilma Rudolph looked a bit lonely. She was an unknown black athlete. Something was seriously wrong with her left leg because she hobbled with a limp. Some observers were asking aloud, "What's she doing here? What is the United States trying to prove?"

It took exactly 11 seconds for the world to find out what Wilma Rudolph was doing in Rome that year. When the starting pistol cracked in the 100-meter dash, Wilma tore up the cinder path in world-record time to capture her first gold medal.

Her second race was the 200-meter dash. No one could figure out why Wilma would even enter this race. Germany's Yetta Hynie was heavily favored to win it. She held the world's record in the event. No one expected to beat Yetta, no one but Wilma Rudolph.

Again, the starting pistol cracked. Wilma and Yetta jumped to a commanding lead, leaving the remainder of the field behind to quarrel among themselves for third place.

As the pair made the turn, the crowd was on its feet screaming wildly. The two raced neck and neck, stride for stride, to the finish line. With a burst of speed on the backstretch, Wilma pushed out to the lead, snapped the victory tape, and captured her second gold medal with a stunning upset of the world champion.

Several days later, Wilma would be competing again against a revenge-seeking Yetta Hynie. But this time the race was the 400-meter relay, and the German foursome, featuring Yetta as the anchor runner, was the heavy favorite. They held the world's record. No one dared to challenge the Germans, no one but Wilma and the Americans.

The starter's pistol cracked, and the first leg of the race began with a burst. Apparently this would be a duel between the Germans and the Americans. The first runners handed the batons cleanly to the second. The second runners made a clean exchange with the third.

Wilma and Yetta were on the anchor leg. When the third runners made the exchange of batons to Wilma and Yetta, Wilma dropped hers, allowing Yetta to coast all alone toward the victory line for what seemed a sure-fire gold medal for the German foursome.

No one knows what happened in that next instant. Perhaps, for a moment, Wilma looked beyond that Roman cinder path; beyond the walls of that stadium, and sent out a cry to her mother back home in Tennessee. And a still, small voice came back . . . "Never give up! Never, never, never give up!"

We do not know if that actually happened, but we do know what Olympic records tell us did happen. Wilma was hopelessly behind. With less than ten seconds to go and less than 100 yards from the finish line, Wilma reached down, picked up the baton in one fist and began her comeback.

She raced neck and neck, stride for stride, to the finish line, 75 yards to go . . . 60 yards to go . . . 25 yards to go. With a burst of speed at the finish, she pushed out to the lead, snapped the tape, and captured her third gold medal. She was the first American woman in the history of the Olympics ever to win three gold medals.

One hundred thousand screaming fans were on their feet yelling wildly because they knew they were not just watching another race; they were witnessing a miracle, the miracle of Wilma Rudolph.

Motivational Therapy

Most motivational speakers who use a lot of self-disclosure seem to benefit emotionally as much from telling their story as the audience does by listening to the story. You may have an experience ideally suited to helping you develop a unique motivational speech. It doesn't mean you have to have an experience like W. Mitchell's or spend seven years as a North Vietnamese prisoner of war like Captain Jerry Coffee, who is another highly sought-after motivational speaker. Your story may be less catastrophic than these, but it might help you build rapport with your audience by sharing with them a piece of your life.

Motivational Quotes

One way to begin using motivation in your presentations is to start with motivational and inspirational quotes from people you admire. Michael personally likes the many good words of the great football coach Vince Lombardi, whose son Vincent is now sharing his late father's message from platforms all over the world.

Another quotable coach is Lou Holtz of Notre Dame football fame, not for what *he* said, but for what was said to him. Michael first met Coach Holtz when he came to the University of South Carolina in Columbia when Head Coach Marvin Bass hired him. Bass got the axe a week later, and Paul Dietzel was hired to build the coaching fortunes for the Gamecocks. Dietzel called Holtz into his office and told him, "Coach Holtz, there is some good news and some bad news. The good news is that we are going to build a great football program here at the University of South Carolina. The bad news is that you are not going to be a part of it."

You might say Holtz got the better end of the deal. Dietzel never accomplished the first half of his mission, but Holtz went on to fame and fortune as a great coach and motivational speaker.

If you are not a football fan, you can find many other sources for quotes, like politics. Teddy Roosevelt, Will Rogers, Winston Churchill, Dame Margaret Thatcher, and John F. Kennedy are just several famous political figures who can provide a cache of quotable material for your motivational message.

The important thing to remember about using a quote is to make sure it has relevance to the point you're making. Do not just quote someone for the sake of quoting them. Use quotes sparingly and with force.

Many speakers like to sandwich their material between quotes, starting a speech off with some inspirational thought and then closing it out with the same inspirational thought. The body of the speech is the "meat" in the sandwich. (See Chapter 9.)

As you become a student of motivation and inspiration, you will want to begin building your own resource library. Another important step you can take is to study how other speakers use quotes. Make mental notes on what you liked or did not like about how the particular speakers integrated the material into their presentation. Before tossing out the quote as a bad idea, make sure you ask yourself the question, "Was it used in correct context?"

Jeff Slutsky likes to quote scenes from movies. For example, when he is describing how a "street fighter" does research to discover what his or her competition is up to, he starts by recalling a scene from the movie *Patton*. In the movie, the night before General Patton is to go against Erwin Rommel for the first time, you see Patton in bed reading a book. He places it by the nightstand before he turns out the light. The title is *Tank Warfare* by Erwin Rommel. The next scene takes place the following morning. Patton is looking through his binoculars and sees Rommel's tanks making their moves. Then Patton's tanks ambush Rommel's tanks and are clearly beating them. Still looking through the binoculars, Patton smiles then shouts, "Rommel, you magnificent bastard. I read your book!"

Other quotes from movies might include a line from the *Wizard of Oz* that deals with abrupt change, "Toto, I don't think we're in Kansas any more." *The Godfather II* supplies a great quote on always knowing what your competition is doing, "My father once told me, 'Michael, keep your friends close, but your enemies closer.'" In *Back to School,* Rodney Dangerfield talks about setting priorities, "Always look out for number one . . . but don't step in number two!"

20 Questions to Help You Develop Your Motivational Speech

To help you begin thinking about your own unique stories to use in developing your motivational speech, spend some time answering the following 20 questions, then follow each with the question "Why?"

1. Is there a parent, brother, sister, or other special relative who inspires me in a particular way?
2. Is there a minister, priest, or rabbi who inspires me?
3. Was there a teacher who motivated or inspired me?
4. Is there a coworker or boss who inspires me?
5. Is there an author who inspires me?
6. Is there a speaker who inspires me?
7. Is there a friend who inspires me?
8. Is there an actor or actress who inspires me?
9. Is there a profession or career that inspires me?
10. Is there a cause that inspires me?
11. Is there a charity that inspires me?
12. Is there an event that inspires me?
13. Is there something that has happened to me that inspires me?
14. Is there an obstacle, hurdle, or disability in my life that inspires me?
15. How can I take this source of inspiration and transfer it into a lesson for others?
16. How do I want them to feel after I have shared this?

17. How can I take legitimate ownership of the material, or do I need to get permission to use it?
18. What do I want my audience to gain from this vignette?
19. What action do I want them to take because of this?
20. How do I want to change their life because of what I shared?

Toastmasters International defines "The Value of Inspiration" in Speech Ten of the *Communication and Leadership Program Manual* as follows:

> We all develop routines, often forgetting what first motivated us toward a particular goal or even what our goals are. For this reason, we periodically need new motivation to help us break out of our routines and set and achieve goals. This need is a challenge for you as a speaker, one you can meet by understanding how to inspire an audience.
>
> Essentially, your purpose in this type of speech is to say what your listeners already think and feel. You're speaking for the audience, putting their sentiments into words appropriate to the occasion. This approach appeals to noble motives and the highest beliefs.

"As you speak," Toastmasters International continues, "you should follow these four essential precepts of leadership:"

1. **Be confident.** Since you're giving expression to something your audience already feels and believes, this isn't the place to raise questions or express doubts.
2. **Be forceful.** Show enthusiasm and vitality. Use body language to demonstrate your conviction. Paint vivid word pictures to bring the audience 'up the mountain' with you.
3. **Be positive.** Bold statements telling the audience what they should do will stir them to action; criticizing them or making excuses for what they have failed to do will not inspire them at all.
4. **Be definite.** Give clear and specific illustrations and conclusions. Present enough information to make sure your audience is with you all the way.

Confidence comes from knowing that you know your material. *"Fear,"* according to Michael Aun's grandfather, Jiddy Mack, "is nothing but an absence of knowledge, a lack of information. Give people the information they need, fear will disappear, and confidence will take over."

Forceful is not about power and authority. In fact, there is great power in humility and softness. Chris Haggerty, CPAE, says that "the strength of the male speaker lay in his ability to show his vulnerability." Enthusiasm is not something that one can manufacture. The word *enthusiasm* comes from the Greek word *ethos* meaning "the spirit within or God within." Enthusiasm comes when a speaker believes in his or her message.

Positive, bold statements identify themselves in the action part of what the statement says. To inspire another, never seek to apologize for your position. Be courageous enough to stand your ground, or do not give the advice.

Being definite in your approach and offering clear and specific illustrations and conclusions is all about preparation. The key to any motivational vignette or speech is to tailor the material to the occasion. To do that, you must know your audience like they do themselves. Understanding what is important to the audience is a key step to creating an effective motivational speech. Understanding what the audience's expectations are is critical to the success of any presentation.

Before constructing your inspirational speech, put as much of yourself into the presentation as you can before spicing it up with quotes and stories about and from others. Essentially, quotes and motivational stories should be the "seasoning" for the meal. The metaphorical meal itself should be what you, the speaker, brings to the table.

There are dozens of speaking opportunities to use such an inspirational or motivational speech. Some include the pregame pep talk, the sales talk, the religious meeting, the holiday function, annual reunions, anniversaries, parent-child banquets, Scout functions, dedications, commencement addresses, and any assemblage that encourages self-improvement like Alcoholics Anonymous, Weight Watchers and other self-help groups.

Techniques of Delivery Are Important

The impact from a motivational speech depends as much on the techniques of delivery than any other kind of presentation. You can absolutely ruin an inspirational speech with poor delivery. You might laugh at the advice, but consider watching a seasoned television evangelist or Wide World of Wrestling pro to get a tip or two. Their impact as presenters has as much to do with performance as with their message. Delivery is the key to making the inspirational/motivational speech flow.

W. Mitchell "looks the part" when he takes the platform. This gives him an advantage in helping him impact his audience even before he speaks. Even so, he tells a captivating story in a very dramatic style, and shortly into his presentation the audience forgets that he's in a wheelchair and that he's severely scarred. Captain Jerry Coffee did the same with his uniform. Upon his return to America, he began traveling around the country sharing his remarkable experience of how he survived by eating bugs and accentuated his story by dressing in his formal white Naval uniform.

When Jerry retired from the Navy, he took off the uniform for his post-Naval presentations and wore a suit. He found this transition difficult at first because he previously had the benefit of the uniform to help set the stage for his delivery. He soon discovered that he didn't need his uniform to connect with his audience. He has a powerful message combined with his poignant speaking style.

☞ **Master's Tips:** *Before you deliver this kind of motivational or inspirational material to any audience, consider the following tips:*

- *Research your topic thoroughly.*
- *Know how you want your audience to feel at the conclusion of your vignette or speech.*
- *Customize and tailor your remarks to the audience.*
- *Make your material relevant to the audience.*
- *Use lots of examples and illustrations.*
- *Uplift the audience's spirits and offer hope for the cause.*
- *Accept yourself for what you are, and try to be more like yourself and less like others.*

Chapter 9

*P*romoting Yourself with Seminar Selling

*O*ne of the most effective promotional tactics for many business people today is *seminar selling,* which uses a seminar to promote your product, service, or idea. The financial services industry has mastered the concept and has turned it into an opportunity to gain credibility and acceptance as well as clients. You can use this approach to sell practically any product or service. This chapter gives you some helpful tips on conducting and promoting your own seminar and thus gain an edge in your sales and marketing efforts.

Seminar Selling Can Cure an Anemic Business

Seminar selling is by no means limited to financial services. This unique approach to public speaking is such a soft sell that it's often used by people who usually aren't considered salespeople, yet may have to market to build their business. For example, Dr. Gary Berebitsky was just starting his pediatrics practice, and he used free seminars to help his practice through infancy (no pun intended). His hospital sponsored prenatal care seminars for expectant mothers, and he taught those seminars free. It was a great public service for both the hospital and Dr. Berebitsky, and both gained new patients because of their effort.

Likewise, a young cardiologist in central Florida used the same technique to build his practice. The only difference was that senior citizens were his target group. He would conduct seminars on ways to reduce the risk of heart attacks and present them at their regular social gatherings. It didn't take more than six months before he was swamped with patients. In both cases, these two doctors used seminars to build their practice in an effective yet very inexpensive manner. Without the use of seminars, they would have had to use more aggressive marketing techniques like newspaper or television advertising, which can be costly and offensive to many potential referring doctors.

Seminar selling is a great vehicle for promoting anything from insurance to incisions. If you have information that your potential customers (or clients, patients, members, etc.) would find valuable, selling via a seminar might be for you. According to Lilly and Dottie Walters, authors of *Speak and Grow Rich* (Prentice-Hall), you need five ingredients for successful seminars:

1. Your seminar must appeal to a specialized market or niche.
2. You must develop a list of good prospects in your market. If you can't identify a large potential audience or potential sponsors of your seminar, you will not have enough buyers to be successful.
3. Your subject must be something that your potential attendees or sponsors want and need.
4. You must be recognized as an authority on your subject.
5. You must develop good marketing skills. Even a "no fee" seminar has to be sold to the sponsor.

The Seminar Versus the Speech

A seminar generally provides you with more marketing benefits than a speech for several reasons: more time, more content, and more audience involvement.

More Time

If you're asked to give an after-dinner talk or speak at a luncheon, you may find that you have only about 30 minutes. The speech is just the entertainment for that particular event. With a seminar, on the other hand, you're more likely to be the event. You don't have to share your audience's time and attention with a meal and the treasurer's report. Also, a seminar generally means that you'll have more time to present your information. A seminar may last as little as an hour, but many can be half-day or even full-day programs.

More Content

The seminar format is better for sharing valuable information. When people attend a seminar, they don't expect to be entertained as much, whereas in a speech they would feel cheated if you couldn't make them laugh. Of course, you don't want to bore them either. But this is not a program where the attendees expect you to provide them with nonstop entertainment. In fact, if you don't provide them with a lot of very useful information in your seminar, you won't achieve your goals. The more they learn about your expertise in the area of the product, service, or idea you represent, the more they are willing to consider it.

More Audience Involvement

A speech is usually a one-way form of communication: You talk; your audience listens. (And if you're lucky, they may even take some notes.) A seminar, conversely, is a format that readily allows for audience participation. By involving your audience in the presentation, you increase their attention on your message. You create involvement through role-playing, exercises, a workbook, or a hand-out that customizes your message to the individual needs of that participant. (See Chapter 4.)

Six Benefits of Seminar Selling

There are many reasons for using a speaking opportunity to promote you, your product, or your service. Seminar selling is more of a soft selling approach that provides many advantages over other forms of more aggressive marketing and selling tactics like telemarketing, advertising, and direct mail campaigns. Following are six of the most obvious benefits of this power approach:

1. Make new contacts and network with existing ones.
2. Educate others about your product, service, or point of view.
3. Strengthen your company's image.
4. Build credibility by positioning yourself as "the expert" in your niche.
5. Motivate others to action.
6. Turn "contacts" into "contracts."

Locating Your Seminar Audience

Before you can give your seminar, you need to find an audience willing to hear your useful information. To acquire a seminar audience, you generally have three options, each carrying a different level of risk:

- existing event
- cosponsored event
- self-promotion

Existing Event

Many organizations have events on their calendar and therefore a built-in audience. Often, the last thing they decide about that event is who will be the speaker. If their event is compatible with providing a two- or three-hour, high-content seminar, you may find this very useful. These types of programs give you the least amount of risk.

Cosponsored Event

Like an existing event, a cosponsored event also is very low risk to you, but it differs with the existing event because it is specifically planned around your seminar. The cosponsor will offer your seminar to their membership, customers, or employees. If they intend to invite the public to the event, the cosponsor generally pays for all the advertising to make people aware of it. In this case, you get the added benefit of having your name in the promotion as well.

Self-Promotion

Self-promotion is the highest risk seminar because you have to pay for all the expenses. This may include the advertising, meeting room rental, refreshments, handouts, and so on. The big advantage of the self-promoted event is that you have complete control over it. You don't have to rely on someone else to promote you who may not be motivated to put in the effort that would generate a good attendance. Plus you don't have to be concerned about anyone else telling you what you can and cannot talk about at your seminar.

The self-promoted seminar is ideally suited for professional salespeople because it's tougher today than ever before to prospect successfully. Salespeople who call on corporations or associations find themselves confronted by what Jeff Slutsky refers to in his book, *Street Smart Tele-Selling: The 33 Secrets* (Prentice-Hall), as the "Dobermans." These impenetrable gatekeepers are specifically hired to keep people like you away from their superiors.

There are also the electronic Dobermans, more commonly referred to as "voice mail," which screen each and every call, not only in the commercial world but at home as well. Salespeople know it's a real challenge to get their phone calls returned.

Sales reps are working harder than ever to prospect, but fewer and fewer are able to even get an audience for their message. Many creative sales professionals have turned to seminar selling for educating prospects about their product or service.

In the Knights of Columbus, Michael Aun's salespeople conduct Members' Benefits Nights to educate their members about the many available membership benefits. The salespeople have found that most members do not know that many free benefits are available to them just for joining, including special values on insurance and annuity products. Using these self-promoted seminars as a marketing tool, the salespeople can educate many members at one time about those special services, which leads to additional sales of insurance products.

The Community-Involvement Seminar

If you're doing self-promoted events, you may want to see if you can find a way to reduce your risk by finding a cosponsor. For example, a financial account executive was spending a great deal of money on advertising to get people to attend his public seminar on investment options for IRAs. Jeff Slutsky suggested to him that he approach an organization like a church and turn that seminar into a fundraiser for them.

The church would promote his seminar, which would be held at their facility. They agreed on what would be considered a *qualified lead,* someone who has a high potential of using the services based on their income, tax bracket, age, and so on. For each qualified participant whom the church motivated to attend the seminar, the account executive would make a $10 donation to the building fund. If they could bring in at least 50 qualified leads, he would donate an additional $100.

Currently, because the financial account executive was using newspaper and radio advertising for his public seminars, leads were costing him over $25 each. Working with a church reduced that cost per qualified lead by half over using newspaper advertising, plus it reduced the risk altogether because he paid only for results. Advertising in the local newspaper didn't have a guarantee.

This approach is what Jeff refers to as "community involvement" in his book *Street Fighter Marketing* (Lexington Books). It's a great way not only to reduce your risk while generating seminar attendees but also to gain a "good guy" image in your marketplace. Once a cosponsor gives you a group of qualified leads, you present that person with a check to his or her cause, which is another opportunity for a little bit of post-publicity.

Promoting Your Seminar

Once you've decided to use a seminar to help sell your product, service, or idea, you have to promote the seminar. Here are some ideas to put on your list of things to do to help make your seminar selling program more successful.

Planning the Details

Be sure to set your program date far enough in advance. The more lead time you have, the more you can effectively plan out every detail of your program. One of the biggest causes of failure in seminar selling programs is poor planning. This can occur because the speaker just doesn't allow enough time to take care of all the little details. Other elements that also need to be determined when selecting your seminar date include location, time of the program, and program length.

Work with a chairperson. For sponsored or cosponsored seminars, usually one person in each group is assigned to help with the details. Make sure that the group with whom you plan to work on your seminar has someone who has agreed to help you with many of the time-consuming tasks. A chairperson can usually help you arrange for a meeting room and your audio/visual requirements, help with promotion of the event, and also help you with registration and other details on the day of the event.

Work with a food chairperson, if possible. Hopefully, the event you are planning involves food. Food is a great incentive to get more people to attend your program. It also takes a great deal more effort. That's why it's very beneficial for you to have that organization assign a chairperson who is responsible for the food. They will deal with the caterer or the volunteers if it's a pot luck dinner. They'll also arrange for the set up, serving, and clean up following the program. Also, plan your meal with flexibility. You always want to be prepared to increase the head count if necessary. Nothing is more frustrating than turning prospects away.

Marketing Your Seminar

Mail out teaser announcements. Starting several months out and leading up to the date of the program, have the group send out "teasers" to remind prospective attendees of your upcoming seminar. Though these reminders are usually postcards, you can also use telephone calls, mentions, or stuffers in the group's regular mailers like newsletters. The more exposure you get for the seminar, the greater your chances of have having a good attendance. After all, you can't sell them if they don't show!

You want to get creative here to make some impact with your potential attendees. Since some form of mailing is likely to be part of your marketing program, you want to do something that really gets attention. One of the biggest problems of most direct mail is getting your advertising message read. Most "junk mail" gets tossed in the trash even before the envelope is opened. So creating mail pieces that at least get looked at puts you way ahead of the pack.

One way to get people to see your advertising message is by putting it on the back of a picture postcard of a vacation spot. Picture postcards get attention because they don't look like advertising. A person receiving a postcard from Disney World, for example, is going to want to know who they know went to Disney World. They'll turn it over and read it. By contrast, most mail advertising is tossed in the garbage unnoticed.

The sure-thing mailer.   Picture postcards can be effective and relatively inexpensive because you can mail them first class for much less than a first-class envelope. Here's an idea that could easily be adapted to promote your seminar from Jeff Slutsky's book *Street Fighter Marketing.* At a printing convention in Las Vegas, a quick printer bought up 400 picture postcards from the MGM Grand. She took them back to her small town in Ohio and had her kids hand-address them with the names of 400 businesses who were not her customers. The headline on the back of the postcard said, "Don't Gamble with Your Printing." It went on to offer a 10 percent savings on their first printing order. She received 100 redemptions on her offer. That's a 25 percent return, which is unheard of in direct mail. Another businessperson was in Orlando and bought postcards from Disney World. His headline read, "Don't Mickey Around with Your Retirement." Of course, the postcards featured Mickey Mouse. He also had some other postcards that read, "If You Think Your Retirement Plan Is Goofy . . ." It received a lot of attention.

The trash to treasure mailer.   One of the more clever direct mail campaigns was used by a REALTOR®. The first mailer was a simple 5½″ × 4¼″ one-color postcard. The postcard was nothing spectacular and got trashed as expected. A week later a standard business envelope arrived to the same homes. Inside the envelope was the same postcard that had been crumpled up and then flattened. Attached to the decrumpled postcard was a handwritten note that read, *"Please don't throw this away again! Thanks!"* The people's first reaction was "How did this guy get this back? Did he go through our trash?" In reality, it was a planned second mailing. It attracted a lot of attention, including a free article in a neighborhood newspaper. The third mailing was a letter. Instead of getting trashed, it got read.

Invitation to new sales. Another type of mail piece that gets high readership is the invitation mailer. When you get a wedding invitation in the mail, for example, you open it. It doesn't look like an ad in any way. Getting that mail piece opened and looked at is half the battle, so if you make your mail piece look just like a wedding invitation, your readership goes up dramatically. Similar to the picture postcard approach, you tie the headline of your offer to the invitation theme: *"We Invite You to a Seminar on Saving Money"* or *"You are Cordially Invited to Learn How to Retire Comfortably."*

To make full impact in your invitation mailer, use the following guidelines.

1. *It is expensive to use an actual wedding invitation but you can achieve the same impression by printing your piece on textured paper, vertical format, 5½" × 8½" folded over to 5½" × 4¼".* That size is printed two to a sheet of paper (*2-up* in printer's talk), so to print 1,000, you need only 500 sheets, cut in half. Your quick printer will have matching envelopes. (This size is referred to as *A-2* or *Baronial.*) If you use a larger size, it will cost you more because it's more custom. *Use an italic type style that resembles a wedding invitation but not one that is so fancy or ornate that it's difficult to read.* You can use raised print if you like (*thermograph*) but offset printing is usually less expensive, is printed on-premises, and should work fine.

    Every once in a while your quick printer or wedding invitation marketer might have an actual wedding invitation style that's discontinued or dramatically reduced in price for one reason or another. It's a long shot but worth checking out. Compare the cost of a real invitation with that of creating your own "mock" invitation. If they're close and the style is impressive, you might consider it if it doesn't have any reference to a "wedding" on the front. Of course, you won't need the return envelopes and extra inserts.

2. *Print in a script-type font somewhat like this, with the return address on the envelope flap but not the company name.* If the customer perceives that it's from a business, you lessen your chance of getting that envelope opened.

3. *Hand address the envelopes.* If you use a label or have them output on a laser printer, you'll lose big impact. The address doesn't have to be done in calligraphy, but that would make even more impact. You can probably hire some students to do this for you or even some seniors at a retirement center.

4. *Use a commemorative stamp.* Do not use a bulk permit number or postage meter. For maximum impact, mail it first class. The ideal stamp is the "LOVE" stamp. That gets attention because LOVE stamps are always used for wedding invitations. Your next choice would be any colorful commemorative stamp. The U.S. Postal Service issues new ones each year, so see which ones are available for you. However, you can make a little extra impact if the stamps happen to have one that also reinforces your product or service. For example, a florist could use flower stamps, a car dealer could use the antique car stamps, a movie theater or video store would use the classic films stamps, a sporting goods store could use the Olympic Games stamps, and so on. It's a nice touch but not critical.

Invite prospects from outside the sponsoring group. This seminar is a great platform for you to show off your "stuff," so get as much mileage out of your effort as possible. If the sponsor permits, invite other potential buyers to your program. This allows you to expand your audience without having to conduct another seminar. It's also valuable if there aren't enough of the others you wish to invite to conduct a separate seminar for them.

Jeff Slutsky and his brother Marc were booked to conduct a half-day seminar on low-cost neighborhood marketing tactics for the Columbus, Ohio, office of Barter Exchange International. This international company has over 150 offices that offer a barter service for small businesses. The seminar was provided for their members as a way to provide useful information. They paid to attend but paid using their barter credits. In addition, both Street Fighter Marketing and BXI Columbus invited nonmembers to the seminar, who had to pay cash. This allowed the Slutsky brothers to expand beyond the membership attendance, which resulted in greater sales of their audio and video programs, plus their consulting projects. BXI Columbus also had the opportunity to expose the nonmembers to their barter program and picked up some new members as a result.

Make formal announcements. At the group's regular meetings, make sure that announcements are made to promote your seminar. If someone in the audience has heard you speak before, you might suggest that during the announcement the emcee ask that person to share several minutes of why he or she thinks it would be a good idea for everyone to attend. This is also a good time to hand out fliers on the seminar as well. If you have a high-energy presentation, you might consider having the organization show a short video of your program. BXI Columbus used Jeff's demo video at several meetings prior to the seminar, and once members saw just five minutes of it, they immediately signed up to attend the seminar.

Send press releases. Publicity can be a powerful tool for creating exposure and interest in your seminar. A simple press release containing the basic information about your seminar should be sent to publications that typically promote the target group's meetings. It's a good idea to develop a list of the publicity outlets in your community that typically mention seminars. This list might include your local daily newspaper, the free suburban papers, specialty papers like your local business journal, radio stations, local cable access, and even some TV stations. This list is something you can use repeatedly for future programs.

When writing your press release, make sure that you are providing the reporter with information that you would want to share with their audience. Reporters are not interested in giving you free publicity. In the headline and first sentence, put all the critical information that answers the questions who, what, when, where, why, and how. Figure 9.1 shows a sample press release to help guide you along on format and content.

FIGURE 9.1   Sample Press Release

(on the sponsor's letterhead)

FOR FURTHER INFORMATION CONTACT:
Jeff Slutsky, President
Streetfighter Marketing
467 Waterbury Court
Gahanna, Ohio 43230
614-337-7474   fax 614-337-2233

FOR IMMEDIATE RELEASE

STREET FIGHTERS CONDUCT SEMINAR
ON LOW-COST ADVERTISING FOR SMALL BUSINESS

COLUMBUS, OHIO—ABC Exchange International is sponsoring a
half-day seminar on low-cost advertising on June 15th at the
Ramada Inn on Morse Road. The seminar will be conducted by
Jeff and Marc Slutsky, who are the authors of several books on
the subject, including *Street Fighter Marketing* and *How to Get
Clients*.

Registration will begin at 7:30 AM, and the seminar will begin
promptly at 8:15 and will end at noon. The cost per person is
$199 with discounts available for multiple attendees from the
same organization. Each attendee will get a complete workbook
and a copy of the Slutskys' first book, *Street Fighting: Low-Cost
Advertising for Your Business.*

To preregister or for additional information about the seminar,
contact Joseph Smith, President of ABC Exchange International
at 614-555-1000.

#######

Target your audience.   Big audiences are nice, but for selling purposes you're concerned with only those attendees who are potential buyers of your product or service. It doesn't hurt to get free publicity to the masses, but you want to narrow your efforts as much as possible. For instance, if what you promote has nothing to do with children, do not encourage their attendance, but do not refuse them if they do happen to attend. Find those publications, mailing lists, organizations, and businesses that cater to your target audience.

Conducting the Successful Selling Seminar

Once you've successfully promoted the seminar so that you have a number of qualified prospects in attendance, you next have to ensure that you present your seminar so that you achieve your sales objectives.

Separate the food time from the seminar time.   Try not to take a break between the program and the meal. Try to have the program first and the meal second. People are more likely to stick around. When serving hors d'oeuvres and refreshments, you might need to provide them first but for a very specific amount of time. Then the food is cleared and the seminar begins.

The shorter the seminar, the better.   The entire program should not exceed two hours. One hour is even better. Use as much time as you need to help the audience understand the value of considering to buy or to buy into what you have. But don't allow your presentation to go any longer than it absolutely has to. With this type of selling, generally "less is more."

Avoid controversial subjects and never knock the competition.   People do not care about your problems. As Cavett Robert, founder of the National Speakers Association and 1949 winner of the Toastmasters International World Championship of Public Speaking, used to say, "Eighty percent of the people don't care about your problems, and the other 20 percent think you deserve them."

Gear your presentation for the audience size.   The smaller the group, the more intimate you need to be. Larger groups might not be appropriate for this kind of program. The ability to ask questions is tougher with a larger audience. If your group is over 50 people, you probably need a microphone and a good sound system. Many professional speakers own their wireless microphone with all the appropriate jacks to get into any sound system. Michael Aun likes using the "Oprah" or "Montel Williams" format of allowing people to ask questions. Jeff Slutsky, on the other hand, usually wears a clip-on wireless and then tells the person asking the question to "talk into my tie," which gets a good chuckle.

Use visual aids.   Proper use of visual aids can dramatically increase the response from your attendees. In a very small group, anything works well from a flip chart to slides to overhead transparencies. In a group of five, you can even use a laptop computer for the presentation if the screen is adequate for all of you to gather around and follow the presentation. For a larger group, you could project a computer presentation on a screen or through a large monitor.

Use handouts, workbooks, brochures, or other take-home materials.   Remember, the attendees like to get information both verbally and in hard copy. Give them what they want—the information you promised that you would give them. Handouts are a wonderful way to also keep your name in front of those who attended. You might even consider using a header or footer where your name, company name, and phone number appear at the top or bottom of every page.

Provide a method for asking questions.   A simple piece of paper and pencil may be good enough. Some people may want to ask questions, but they are not comfortable asking their question in front of the group or feel that their question might cause them embarrassment. Taking questions on paper or index cards during the breaks gives the attendees a safe way to participate.

Be entertaining.   Entertainment does not replace the important information you will give your audience, but you'll generally get a better result if you include it. As we saw in previous chapters,

the entertainment element in your seminar may involve any combination of humor, audience participation, props, dramatic stories,
video clips, and perhaps even other special talents you have that
you can weave into your presentation. Just make sure that whatever you do to increase the entertainment value of your program
enhances your message and never takes away from it.

Be industry or product specific.   Don't ramble. Start with
a good strong outline of all the key points you want to cover. Stick
with *your* subject, not someone else's. Remember your purpose
in being in front of this group. When you veer away from your subject matter, not only do you lose your audience; you could be ven-
turing into dangerous territory, offering opinions on matters on
which you might not be qualified.

Master your subject.   The late Earl Nightingale, a recipient
of the prestigious Golden Gavel Award presented by Toastmasters
International, once suggested, "If you devote one hour of study per
day to your particular subject, in five years, you will be a foremost
expert on that subject." So know your material. Your entire credibility hinges on the validity and profundity of what you have to say.

Be honest with your audience.   If you do not know an answer to a question, do not try to "wing it." Tell them that they have
a valid question, and you will be happy to get the answer and get
back to them; or perhaps ask if anyone present can enlighten the
group on the answer. Remember the thoughts of the great speaker
Christopher Haggerty, another member and a frequent presenter
at Toastmasters International, who said, "The great strength of our
species is in his or her ability to show their vulnerability." Do not
try to know everything. Your ability to show humility can become
a terrific strength, especially if someone is trying to sandbag you
with a "trick" question. The best way to disarm them is to be absolutely honest and humble.

If you don't understand the question, you may have to get addi-
tional information before you decide if you can provide an answer.
You might follow up with, "That's a very interesting question.
Why do you ask it?"

Follow up with your attendees. At the end of your seminar, ask your attendees to fill out a brief evaluation form. This helps you get their opinions about the seminar. The following questions are nonthreatening and can provide you with a wealth of information:

1. What did you like most about our program?
2. If you could change just one thing about the program that would have made it better for you, what would that be?
3. If you were putting on a program like this, what would you add?

These questions are not aggressive and are genuinely seeking information that can help you in your next seminar. They also can provide you with tremendous insight into what interests these particular prospects most.

You will have to remind your attendees to take a moment to fill out the evaluation forms for you. They can then fold them in half and leave them on a back table. You can also have an optional place at the bottom for their name and address. This is useful in getting quotes for your future advertising pieces. On the form you can ask, "May we have permission to quote you for marketing future programs? Yes. No. (circle one)."

Watch your manners, your humor, and your stories. Never insult or hurt anyone, intentionally or unintentionally. Be careful that the stories you use are not inappropriate for the group. Don't be afraid to use humor to make points about serious matters, but just make sure the humor is appropriate.

"Casualness leads to casualties," according to the great speaker and author Jim Rhon. One very important element is to leave nothing to chance. "Trust no one," says Joel Weldon. He shows up hours before a presentation to make sure that everything is in order. He quips, "I like everyone involved, but I trust no one." He makes sure that his room setup is correct because he sets it. He makes sure that the audiovisual is operating because he is there to make sure that it is operating. He makes sure that the environment is the way he wants it.

The Anatomy of a Seminar Outline

Developing an outline for both a seminar or speech is similar, but the seminar outline requires much more detail. You build your seminar outline in layers starting from the basic points and building outward. A speech outline, on the other hand, might list only the key points and perhaps a second level of detail. (See Figure 9.2.)

The primary points of the outline should be the key concepts or ideas that you want your audience to take out of your program. After all, you *do* want them to take action on your ideas, whether you are making a presentation to the PTA for a new playground or doing an evaluation to your fellow NASA engineers to seek funding for new technology for the space shuttle.

Start with a basic, bare-bone draft, laying out the ideas in the order in which you wish to deliver them. This is your *skeleton*. Once your original draft is in writing, then go back and add in "your" personal thoughts, research, findings, support material, and illustrative anecdotes. This is the *muscle* that goes over the skeleton. Next, you need transitions or segues to smoothly connect one key point to another. These serve as the *tendons* of your presentation. Though not on your written outline, the final element you add to this anatomy is your presentation style, which would be analogous to the *skin* that covers the rest.

The beauty of Toastmasters International is that you learn how to organize your presentation. Toastmasters International evaluates "why" you should organize a speech and helps you in creating the talk. One of the primary focuses of this particular project in the manual is to complete an outline. Any good speech should be constructed much like a sandwich. The top piece of bread represents your opening. The meat of the sandwich is your thoughts. The bottom piece of bread is your closing. Your third speech in the Toastmasters International *Communication and Leadership Program* manual deals with "Organizing Your Speech."

FIGURE 9.2 Speech Versus Seminar Outline Format

Speech Outline Format
1. Key Point
   a. _____
   b. _____
   c. _____
2. Key Point
   a. _____
   b. _____
   c. _____

Seminar Outline Format
1. Key Point
   a. _____
      i. _____
      ii. _____
        (1) _____
        (2) _____
   b. _____
      i. _____
        (1) _____
        (2) _____
        (3) _____
      ii. _____
      iii. _____
   c. _____
      i. _____
      ii. _____
        (1) _____
          (i.) _____
          (ii.) _____
          (iii.) _____
        (2) _____
2. Key Point
   a. _____
      i. _____
      ii. _____
   b. _____
      i. _____
      ii. _____
      iii. _____
   c. _____
      i. _____
      ii. _____
        (1) _____
        (2) _____

The Opening of Your Presentation

Any good presentation starts with a strong and fast opening. Here are a few suggestions from Toastmasters International:

Use a startling question or a challenging statement to capture the audience. An example to a group listening to a banker address the importance of saving money to send a child to college might be: "How many of you can afford to send your child to college right now?" Jeff Slutsky often opens his speech, "Confessions of a Marketing Street Fighter" with the question, "By show of hands, how many people here today are street fighters?" Since very few raise their hands, he continues, "Well, what is a street fighter? Perhaps I can illustrate for you what a street fighter is with an example." And then he launches into one of his signature stories on marketing and sales.

Use an appropriate quotation, illustration or story. This is a great way to segue into what you wish to say. Someone doing a eulogy for a friend at a funeral might start with an appropriate quote. For example, at one eulogy, Michael quoted the seventeenth-century poet John Donne, "No man is an island entire to himself . . . and therefore, never send to know for whom the bell tolls, it tolls for thee."

Display some object or prop to "break the ice." Perhaps a videotape on some particular topic might be a great way to introduce the rest of your talk. Jim Cathcart, CSP, CPAE, shows his audience an acorn to begin his signature story, which compares employees to types of trees. His fable tells of a proverbial "oak tree" that management told to become more like a "redwood."

The Body of Your Presentation

The "meat" of your speech is the most important part of the presentation. The body, or content, contains the factual support of your presentation. The amount and depth of information you are able to share is limited by the time you have available to tell it. Toastmasters International suggests three keys to the body: a statement of facts, proof of your presentation, and, if appropriate, a refutation of contrary views. The body is your chance to sing. It is your opportunity to sell your topic and close the audience on your thinking.

*T*oasting a *M*aster
BILL GOVE

---

*B*ill Gove of Atlantis, Florida, is a master at the process of building a speech. Bill was the first president of the National Speakers Association and, like Cavett Robert, was a winner of Toastmasters International's Golden Gavel Award. Before retiring to Florida, Bill was one of the most sought-after keynote speakers in the world. He has delivered thousands of presentations in scores of countries all over the world.

Bill is a master at using vignettes to build a speech. A *vignette* is an anecdote, or series of related anecdotes, within the speech or seminar. In a way, it's like a mini-speech within the speech. It contains all the same ingredients of a speech: an opening, a body, and a closing. Each vignette is designed to segue to the next, tying the presentation together with a series of stories that are closely correlated to an overall theme.

Bill could "build" a speech geared to the needs of the audience and the time available using any combination of his vignettes. Though each of these segments contained Bill's standard stories, the unique combination he used for each seminar allowed him to tailor his presentation without having to develop a completely new one.

Using an acronym.   Some speakers prefer to design their speeches around an acronym, such as S-U-C-C-E-S-S, with each letter representing a particular point that they are making in the speech. This tool can help you keep on track, give the audience some idea of the sequence of events, and uniquely tie the entire presentation together.

This clever use of a word to build a speech is used quite often, but again it must be relevant. Be prepared to shorten the material if your time is changed because of other speakers or events going over their allotted time.

The Closing of Your Presentation

The conclusion of your presentation should lead up to a climax because that's exactly what it is—the destination at which you hope to leave your audience. This is where your speech should produce results.

Toastmasters International teaches that your conclusion should always tie into your opening and your body, and it should leave no doubt about what you want the audience to do with the information you have delivered to them. The conclusion should also be forceful and confident. A weak or inconclusive closing is almost apologetic in nature and can kill even the best speech.

The best closing revisits the material covered in the speech, summarizing the points you made in your original outline and the conclusions you reached. The closing is also an opportunity to appeal for action. A story or a quotation is a great way to illustrate the major focus of the speech.

Take care to do your "housekeeping" material prior to your final story or closing line. This is where you thank the sponsors and your chairperson. Then tell your closing story or quote so you leave the audience on a high note.

Meeting Room Setup and Dynamics

If you have any control of the room, some elements that might help you get better results. Keep the room just a little on the cool side, around 68 to 70 degrees. Once the room fills up with people, it will get warm and it's much more difficult working with people in a warm room. This is particularly important if your presentation follows a meal.

If your audience members will be doing a lot of writing, set your room up classroom style with tables. If they will not, you will be better off theater style. With either approach, consider having it set up *chevron* style, in which the chairs and tables are set up in a "V." This makes it easier for the people in the outer rows to participate.

When you don't know how many people will attend your presentation, you might end up with half the seats empty. Most people will likely sit in back. To avoid this problem, set up fewer rows, but have extra chairs available, stacked in the back of the room. You can then add chairs in the back, as needed. This also creates a different atmosphere when, at the last minute, you're dragging chairs out to accommodate all the people.

Although some may argue that it gives the impression that you're not organized enough to anticipate the crowd, from a marketing point of view, it gives the impression that the turnout was so overwhelmingly successful that you had to put out more chairs at the last minute. This last-minute craziness to get the chairs up actually adds to the energy of the room. No problem in starting five or even ten minutes late. But you may want to make an announcement to the group that you will be starting in five minutes so that the latecomers can get settled.

Since most rooms are rectangular, Tom Winninger suggests that the speaker presents from the long wall, not the short wall like most people do (see Figure 9.3). Because it's much more difficult for the people in the back of the room to see, setting up on the long wall means that the longest distance from you to the farthest person is much less. Set the lectern (and risers if they're used) on the opposite wall or farthest long wall from the entrance to the room. Keep water and displays in the back, except those items you will be demonstrating during your presentation.

If you use a microphone, double check sound quality and room acoustics. Nothing can kill a presentation faster than feedback or a microphone that makes funny noises. When using a wireless microphone, have a wired mike on standby just in case you start getting air traffic control instructions through the sound system. For wired mikes, have enough cord on the mike to move around if that's your style.

Leave nothing to chance. If phones are in the room, have them disconnected. If servers are taking plates, make sure that they know not to do so when you start. Talk to the meeting planner and the person in charge of the room days in advance, and go over your room requirements. Make sure they understand. Draw diagrams if need be. Go to the meeting at least an hour ahead of time to deal with last-minute problems that invariably come up.

FIGURE 9.3 The Long Wall Setup Brings Your Audience Closer to You

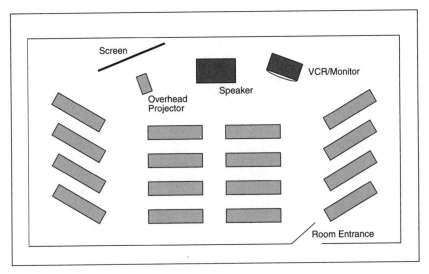

Evaluate Yourself

The best way to improve your speaking skills is through evaluation. That, again, is the beauty of Toastmasters International. You have the golden opportunity to get weekly feedback on your presentation.

Many speakers record their presentation so they can do a "postmortem" on it. This allows you to hear how it sounded, and you'll probably be able to make important improvements with little effort.

☞ **Master's Tip:** *Think of several powerful anecdotes or quotes you could use to incorporate into your closing. Try the different ones out, preferably in front of an audience, and then choose the one that you think will leave the audience strongly motivated to take action.*

Delivering Specialized Presentations

Specialized presentations are some of the most challenging types of presentations you may be asked to deliver. Each of the eight most common types of specialized presentations requires special skills and exceptional effort to give effectively. A Master of Ceremonies' job is far different from the man who is receiving an award or the woman who is nominating a candidate for a particular office.

Besides oratorical competence, you need some particular skills to properly deliver these types of specialized presentations. In this chapter, you will discover important aspects of those roles and how to deal with each.

Below are eight general areas of specialized speaking that this chapter addresses:

1. the roast
2. the toast
3. the invocation
4. the acceptance speech
5. the testimonial
6. the nomination speech
7. the master of ceremonies
8. the eulogy

The Roast

Roasts and toasts have so much in common that both are covered in this chapter. Both the roast and the toast have the same effect. They are ways to show one's affection for the persons being honored and usually have some fun with them at the same time.

Dozens of occasions are perfect for a roast or a toast, but the most common occasion for a toast is generally the personal family event such as a wedding, birthday, anniversary, engagement party, or holiday function. The roast generally takes place when someone is retiring, going away, or promoted, or something significant has happened in the life of the person being honored. In some cases, you may want to use both.

Rules for Roasting

A *roast* is an event where several friends of the person to be honored give a brief, humorous, satirical, and generally good-natured lampoon about that person. The pseudoinsults are fun, and everyone attending—the roaster, the roastee, and the audience—understands that everything said is "tongue in cheek" and that it is truly an honor for the honoree to brave this gauntlet of insights and insults.

Assign a farce enforcer.   You have great flexibility when you structure a roast, but a good guideline might be to have a master of ceremonies (emcee) who keeps things going, in reasonably good taste, and coordinates the event. This person can be a roaster as well, but you may find that the emcee gets a better response by using his or her roasting material between roasters as transition. The other duty of the emcee at a roast is to introduce each roaster, which gives the emcee the unique opportunity of roasting the roaster. This keeps the material from becoming too one sided.

Keep tight time tables.   You want to keep the number of roasters to a manageable number. You'll probably want a minimum of three or four and a maximum of eight or nine. Each roaster should be allotted between five and ten minutes. It's very important that a roaster can stretch five minutes of good material into ten minutes. It's always best to leave your audience wanting more instead of wishing that someone would pull the plug on this roaster. Remember, you want every presentation to be enjoyable, funny, and in reasonably good taste.

Outline an absurdity itinerary.   There are many different formats, but you might want to use this one as a starting point for planning your roast. First, you want the guest(s) of honor to sit up front, but a little off to the side. For a more formal roast, in a banquet room, you should have a riser at the front of the room, with a head table and a lectern in the center. All the roasters sit at the head table with the guest of honor next to the lectern. For a less formal event, you still want to have a lectern and the guest of honor somewhere up front, but the roasters can be in the audience, preferably in the front row.

The emcee opens with some comments about the purpose of the roast and can use a few roasting lines. Then the emcee introduces the first roaster. Once all of the roasters are finished, the guest of honor is then invited to make a rebuttal and gets an opportunity to express his or her "appreciation." Although the material from the emcee, the roasters, and the rebuttal from the guest of honor is supposed to be good-natured ribbing, it's usually a good idea to end each roast with a line or two that is from the heart and expresses love and good wishes.

Roasting a Master: the Michael LeBoeuf Wedding

When Michael LeBoeuf married Elke Stevens, his fellow speaker, friends decided to give him a roast right after the rehearsal dinner. Planning this event started a month earlier, with the main participants using the phone to review their lines. The emcee and best man was your humble coauthor, Jeff Slutsky. Other roasters were all professional speakers as well.

What made this roast a tremendous success was that all the participants used a lot of original humor specific to Michael, but the anecdotes, jokes, and jibes, were delivered so that everyone in the audience could understand them. Too often, roasting is done with inside information, which is funny only to those people who know the guest of honor well. However, when the material is presented properly, the spouses and those who might not personally know the honoree understand the humor and enjoy the evening as well.

For example, quite a few lines referred titles of Michael's various books, but each roaster delivered their material as if the audience knew nothing of Michael's great success.

Michael gave a hilarious rebuttal and then ended on a serious note, "Elke and I have received many great gifts, and we can't begin to express our appreciation of your generosity. However, the best gift we could have received was having all of you come here from all over the country to share this very special time with us. We thank you." It was a perfect ending to a perfect evening, and it also gave Jeff the line he needed to give the first toast to the bride and groom the next day at the reception.

The Toast

At the reception, after a brief fanfare played, the announcer bellowed, "Ladies and gentlemen, may I present for the very first time, Mr. and Mrs. Michael LeBoeuf!" Everyone stood and applauded as Michael and Elke entered the room and took their seats at the head table. Next, Jeff gave his toast:

> Perhaps one of the most exciting duties of the best man is to give the first toast. I know that Michael in particular was very excited when entering the room today because, in 20 years of professional speaking, this was his first standing ovation. You know, last night at the "awards banquet," Michael told us just how much he and Elke appreciated all of you being with them on this day. In fact, he said that your attendance here was the best gift we could have given him. I just wish he had told me that four weeks ago, before I dropped 300 bucks on a piece of crystal. But be that as it may, everyone now, please lift your glass and join me in wishing Michael and Elke a long and happy life together.

A *toast* is a pledge of good intentions, a wish for good health and good things to come to someone or some couple or group. "Eloquence," as the late Ken McFarland, who is considered one of the premier speakers of the first half of the twentieth century, would put it, "is thought on fire." We have to have eloquence in our toasts, and they must have a touch of class about them. A toast should seize the moment. It should offer the audience a hallmark for the occasion, something to take away and remember. It can come as a clever story about the person or some humor that makes a point.

Keep it clean.   Off-color material is inappropriate for this type of occasion. After all, you are there to elevate the subjects to a higher level. Why pull the occasion down with poor taste?

Beware of alcohol.   The very nature of many occasions introduces alcohol as part of the festivities. If you are speaking, avoid the booze. It thickens the tongue and will cause you and your subjects embarrassment. Most of us have a tough enough time speaking when we are stone sober. To throw booze into the mix makes the occasion impossible.

Suit the toast to the occasion.   These are usually happy events. The exceptions are those retirement parties where someone has been forced out of a company. Be sensitive to these *second tier* issues so that the event does not become a bashing of the company or the subject of the roast.

☞ **Master's Tips for a Good Toast or Roast:** *Below are some helpful hints in preparing for your toast or roast:*

1. *Know the time restraints going in, and suit your comments to the time provided.*
2. *Try to personalize your comments.*
3. *Quotes are excellent tools to make your points.*
4. *There is always room for humor at these occasions, as long as it is appropriate and relative.*
5. *Humility is the order of the day. After all, the toast is a pledge of good intentions and best wishes for those being toasted.*
6. *Sincerity is the most important singular attribute of your toast. Believe in what you are sharing.*

The Invocation

One of the most delicate specialized presentations that you might be called to deliver is the invocation, benediction, or blessing over a meal.

There is always someone out there who will take umbrage with something you might say. As a speaker, you do not want to give anyone cause to take offense. You should be politically sensitive to the group to whom you are speaking. Avoid using names that you know would offend. In short, when in Rome, speak as the

Romans do. The use of the names Jesus, Lord, and Divine Master might offend someone. If Michael Aun is speaking to a group of Knights of Columbus members, all of whom are Catholic, he has no problem using the name of God, Jesus, or any other term that might dignify what they believe. On the other hand, when he's speaking to his local Toastmasters Club, he would look for prayers that avoid the use of such names or titles. Why run the risk of offending someone who does not share your belief system?

Here's a prayer used at a meeting that came from ancient Sanskrit verse:

Look to this day, for it is the very life of life. In its brief course lies all the verities and realities of your existence: the glory of action, the bliss of growth, the splendor of beauty. For yesterday is but a dream, and tomorrow is only a vision. But today, well lived, makes every yesterday a dream of happiness and every tomorrow a vision of hope. Look well therefore to this day.

The thoughts are pure and they should offend no one. Another thought-provoking verse Michael uses comes from his favorite Greek author, Anonymous.

Be big enough to admit your shortcomings;
Brilliant enough to accept praise without becoming arrogant;
Tall enough to tower above deceit;
Strong enough to accept criticism;
Compassionate enough to understand human frailties;
Wise enough to recognize your mistakes;
Humble enough to appreciate greatness;
Staunch enough to stand by your friends; and
Human enough to be thoughtful of your neighbors.

The prayer challenges us on a personal level without invoking any higher cause. You can also use quotable lines for prayers. For instance, the writer John H. Rhoades inked the following lines, quoted from time to time:

Do more than exist, live.
Do more than touch, feel.
Do more than look, observe.
Do more than read, absorb.
Do more than hear, listen.
Do more than think, ponder.
Do more than talk, say something.

Challenging and to the point, this verse makes you think about the statements made. The thoughts provided, though, should never be offensive.

Being sensitive to the political and religious beliefs of others should not preclude you from quoting the Bible or religious verse. One of Michael's favorite prayers is the prayer of St. Francis. And if you simply delete the words *Lord* and *Divine Master,* you can use the verse anywhere and no one should take offense. It goes like this:

> Lord, make me an instrument of your peace. Where there is hatred, let me sow love. Where there is injury, pardon. Where there is doubt, faith. Where there is despair, hope. Where there is darkness, light. Where there is sadness, joy. Oh, Divine Master, grant that I might not so much seek to be consoled as to console, to be understood as to understand, to be loved as to love. For it is in giving that we receive. It is in pardoning that we are pardoned. And it is in dying that we are born into eternal life.

This beautiful prayer is often used as a foundation for Michael's customer service programs. In fact, he calls it the "customer service" prayer and he paraphrases much of the verse to make certain points in his presentation.

The English theologian John Wesley's thoughts can make a very powerful invocation:

Do all the good you can,
By all the means you can,
In all the ways you can,
In all the places you can,
At all the times you can,
To all the people you can,
As long as ever you can.

☞ **Master's Tips for Selecting a Prayer:** *Here are ten tips about selecting a prayer for an occasion:*

1. *Suit the prayer to the occasion.*
2. *Know the audience. When in Rome . . .*
3. *Choose a prayer that relates to the purpose of the meeting.*

4. *Be brief. Prayers should be under 60 seconds, but don't speed through the them. Well-timed pauses can be very effective.*

5. *It is okay to use prayers that might come from a particular faith or belief. Nullify the opposition by eliminating words that some might find offensive.*

6. *Be sensitive to men and women in the audience.*

7. *Make sure the prayer is written out so that you will not embarrass yourself by misquoting the author.*

8. *If you take literary license, state it at the outset by saying "I want to paraphrase the prayer of St. Francis . . ." or "to parallel the thoughts of John Wesley . . ." or "to borrow from the words of . . ."*

9. *Remember that prayer is a tradition of those who follow certain belief systems. Do not try to force a prayer onto an audience. Respect their right not to agree with you.*

10. *Prayer should set the tone for the event or function, not replace it. Stand up, speak up and hush up!*

Testimonials

Testimonials, like prayers, should suit the occasion. Be sure to make your testimonial sincere and to the point. When you ramble, you will take away from that to which you are offering testimony.

Webster's Dictionary defines "testimony" as: "1) affirmation; 2) evidence." It goes on to define "testimonial" as: "1) certificate of character, ability, etc.; 2) a tribute given by a person expressing regard for recipient."

The most powerful word used in *Webster's* definitions is "evidence." Do not say something about someone or some issue that is not true or is debatable. Testimonials are like resumes because you want to show the best of the person you are honoring, yet you want to be truthful. For example, if you were to say, "He's a dedicated family man," when half the town knows he has three girlfriends on the side, you will lose credibility. However, you could say if true, "He's a person who always provides for his family." This is less likely to raise eyebrows.

Testimonials are a very common form of public speaking that almost everyone from time to time is called to do. It could be anything from an endorsement of the purchase of new choir gowns at the local church to the finance committee to testifying in court about the character of someone charged with a crime.

☞ **Master's Tips on Testimonials:** *The following are ten thoughts about offering a testimonial:*

1. *It must ring true or it nullifies itself.*
2. *Organize your thoughts before standing and speaking on an issue. A 3" × 5" card is great. List the main ideas in the sequence in which you wish to deliver them.*
3. *When speaking on behalf of a person, be sure to use his or her name often and with sincerity.*
4. *When speaking to an issue, be sure to sell the benefits of the issue being discussed.*
5. *Do not ramble. State your points briefly and sit down. The worst thing you could do when offering a testimonial is to speak too long. The longer you speak, the more credibility you lose. Brevity is the order of the day.*
6. *Never speak against the other side of the issue being debated. Speak in favor of your particular person or idea. You do not strengthen the weak by weakening the strong.*
7. *Give examples that provide further credibility about the issue.*
8. *Appeal to the "buying side" of your audience by selling the benefits of the person or issue.*
9. *Where possible, use examples or visuals to make your points.*
10. *Be brief. Stand up, speak up, and hush up!*

The Acceptance Speech

The key element in giving a successful acceptance speech is *humility*. When you have won an award or have been elected to a position, arrogance, pomposity, or even the slightest display of conceit can destroy the rapport you have with your audience. Let others tell the audience how great you are while you express your appreciation for this recognition or excitement for the opportunity to lead the group.

If you are aware that a speech of this nature is in order, it is always helpful to have your thoughts organized in advance. Sometimes you are caught completely by surprise and find yourself speechless. That should never happen to anyone. Consider committing a quote or two to memory that you can "go to" to suit an occasion.

What happens if the shoe is on the other foot? What happens if you come in second or if someone else is promoted ahead of you? Have some "face-saving" thoughts in that area to go to as well.

Since Michael Aun has had a wealth of experience in his lifetime in losing, he considers himself a far better expert at accepting defeat than he does in being gracious in victory. For example, he lost the race for the South Carolina House of Representatives in 1980. A close and dear friend who knew of Michael's impending defeat came to him the day before the election. He said that people would be looking at Michael to see how he would deal with defeat. Michael congratulated his opponent and wished him the best of luck with all the special challenges ahead for him. He also urged his supporters to support his opponent when possible where they agreed and to stick to their beliefs where they didn't. Michael was as eloquent in defeat as his opponent was in victory.

When Michael won the *Toastmasters International World Championship of Public Speaking* in Vancouver in 1978, he spoke about his previous disqualification in Toronto the year before because he went eight seconds over his allotted time. Then he closed with the observation, "You have to go through Toronto to get to Vancouver." That one line offered humility to his victory speech.

☞ Master's Tip on Acceptance Speeches:

- *Be prepared. Have a quick quote to go to when words fail you.*
- *Thank those who made the occasion possible.*
- *Seek humility. Find a way to give others credit.*
- *Be brief. Nothing irritates audiences more than a "gloater."*
- *Give credit where credit is due. Thank those who made it possible for you to be there.*

- *There may be people in your audience who are very hurt that they were not selected and you were. You must find a way to pay homage to them. It is the gracious thing to do and the perfect occasion to show them respect.*
- *Look for the humor in the occasion. Be sure to make yourself the target of any humor. When Dale Irvin received the coveted CPAE from the National Speakers Association (NSA), he was fourth to give an acceptance speech. Everyone before him, as part of their acceptance, thanked God. When Dale got up he said, "First of all, I want to thank God. Mainly because everyone else has, and I don't want to be the one to tick him off."*

The Nomination Speech

If you are ever called on to nominate someone for a position or an award in an organization, ask yourself the question, "Am I the most appropriate person to handle this task?" Will you do the nomination more harm than good? Part of what the audience is buying with the package is "you." Make sure you bring something to the table beside your good looks and a clever presentation.

Do not overstate the nominee's credentials or attributes. Granted, you can say good things about a nominee that the nominee can't easily say. However, the audience perceives your comments about the nominee as the nominee's anyway.

A nomination presentation also has plenty of room for humor, provided that you make the nominee the target. People appreciate a little self-degradation. It reminds us of the need to be humble.

Stick to the facts in the nomination and keep it brief. Make sure the nominee deserves the comments and that they are accurate. Your opinion is okay, but temper it with your personal experiences about the nominee. Do not offer observations that you have not personally experienced about that person.

Sincerity is singularly the most important attribute of a great nomination speech. If you do not believe the things you are saying about the nominee, your tone of voice and delivery will betray you every time.

☞ **Master's Tips for a Good Nomination Speech:**

- *Know the exact period in which your nomination must fit. Nothing is worse than "getting the hook" for a long-winded nomination.*
- *Know the facts about the nominee. Do not make statements that you cannot verify.*
- *Never make promises for the nominee. Your role is to place the nominee before the group for consideration. Let the nominee support his or her position on his or her own.*
- *Sell, do not tell, the audience on the nominee.*
- *Make sure to clear your comments and observations about the nominee with him or her in advance.*
- *Be sure to write out your thoughts so you will not ramble.*
- *Look for the opportunity to introduce some humor into your presentation.*
- *Be sincere. If you do not believe what you are saying, there is precious little chance that the group will believe what you are saying.*

The Master of Ceremonies

A demanding assignment for any speaker is serving as a master of ceremonies. You got a brief taste of the duty of the emcee in the roast section at the beginning of this chapter. Your primary responsibility as an emcee is to take control of the program. This means that you make sure all the events start and stop on time. To a degree, it is not too dissimilar to the way a talk show host would introduce guests or commercials or interrupt when things get out of hand. So as an emcee, your speaking ability is less important than your talents as a charming sergeant at arms.

You Are Not the Focus

A major potential mistake made by the emcee is to think that he or she is the principal speaker for the occasion. While your verbal skills are important to moving the program along, it is more important that you do your job of conducting the program in a timely fashion.

The dufus on the dais.   Jeff Slutsky was once on a five-person panel to discuss aspects of being a full-time professional speaker. Audience members wrote down their questions on index cards, which were then handed to the emcee. The five panelists were all very experienced, full-time professional speakers. The emcee asked the question, but first he gave his opinions and advice before allowing the five panelists to speak. However, the audience didn't care about the emcee's advice. He forgot his purpose in being there, which was first to introduce each panelist, then to ask the questions for the audience members. As a result, he wasn't invited back to serve as an emcee.

You're the podium policeperson.   The toughest yet most critical task you may have to do is to politely stand and join the speaker at the lectern when he or she goes over the allotted time. The job of the master of ceremonies is much like a show producer. However, you must also be flexible. Things go wrong at banquets; there are usually delays. If you are involved in the planning process of a program, build in some time for delays. If a speaker is scheduled for 20 minutes, you might build an extra five to ten minutes of downtime into the program.

Your Program Agenda

Introduce yourself and your responsibilities.   Your first task is to begin the program by introducing yourself, if someone else has not, and tell the audience who you are and what your role is during the evening. Do not apologize for the role. They appreciate that somebody is in charge.

Introduce your participants.   After you make the suitable introductions of your head table (before or after the meal), it is appropriate to let the audience know what they can expect from the event. This not only gives them an indication of the format, but it also will give them a chance to go to the washroom at the proper time so that your program will not face unnecessary interruptions. You should build in time for washroom and smoking breaks. Most functions today are smoke-free, so give the smokers a chance to take a break.

Falling behind schedule.   What if something goes wrong and you fall behind? One smart thing you can do is to inform the audience of the problem and how you intend to fix it. "Ladies and gentlemen, the kitchen advises us that we will be 20 minutes behind in our meal tonight. With that in mind, and with your permission, I would like to introduce the head table and take care of some other business. When the meals arrive, we will recess to eat. Starting with the head table, to my left . . ."

Nothing irritates an audience more than delays. The longer the delays, the more irritated they get. Get the ball rolling, but save your big guns for the appropriate slot. If you have a keynote speaker, let the speaker's presentation come after the meal. If you have awards to give out or recognition plaques for the outgoing officers, get that kind of business out of the way while you are waiting for the food.

There will be circumstances where you may even have to make presentations while your audience is eating. Groups value recognition as well they should. If you have people to recognize, it is okay to do it during the meal. Your audience will appreciate that you are using their time wisely. The recipients of this praise and attention also will feel less awkward as well.

If you precede the meal with an invocation or a pledge of allegiance, be sure to accomplish this before you get into the rest of your preliminaries. As you progress through your program, remember to be thinking ahead at all times.

Be on your toes if someone is late or cancels unexpectedly. Have a backup plan in place. For example, at Michael LeBoeuf's roast, where Jeff Slutsky was the emcee, one of the roasters was unable to attend because of illness. Jeff made sure that her material was faxed to the hotel, and he found someone else to deliver it. He then made sure that the audience was aware of the circumstances for the change. They were very forgiving for the replacement.

☞ Master's Tips for the Master of Ceremonies:

- *Know your head table—who they are, where they are seated, and exactly what you plan to say about each one of them. Nothing is more embarrassing than introducing the woman next to the speaker as his wife when she isn't.*

- *Take control early and retain control. Remember, you are in charge.*
- *Be flexible. Things happen that are beyond your control. Remember, you cannot control what happens to you, but you can control what you choose to do about it.*
- *Do not be afraid to begin the program if the meal is late and recess to eat when the food arrives.*
- *Do not upstage the dais. You are there to help complement the program, not replace it.*
- *There is a place for humor in your job. Look for the humor of the moment and incorporate it, especially if things have gone wrong.*
- *Make the audience partners to your effort. If you are having trouble getting people to be quiet, use this line in a normal tone of voice: "Would all of those who can hear me, please join me in saying Shhhhhhhhhhhhhhhhhhhhh!" The group will quietly get the message, and you do not have to scream and yell or bang on glasses.*
- *Be sure to let the audience know the rules of engagement. If you plan a break for smoking or the washroom, let them know when it is appropriate to excuse themselves.*

The Eulogy

The eulogy is a very emotional *specialized presentation* that you may be asked to deliver. What makes it tough is the rarity and sadness of the occasion. Unless you are a minister (whose job it is to eulogize the deceased) or the vice president of the United States (whose job it is to attend funerals and say good things about other heads of state), you may rarely be called on to do a eulogy.

However, when the occasion occurs, you must prepare for it. Michael Aun was called upon on three separate occasions in his life to present a eulogy. The first was in 1984 at his mother's funeral. The second was in 1995 when his sister-in-law died at the young age of 40. In both of these instances, he had personal knowledge about the deceased and could incorporate many personal stories. In fact, the eulogy was a celebration of the lives of his mother, Alice Aun, and his sister-in-law, Julie Thiel.

His mom had given birth to 11 children, and 650 people attended her funeral to pay her homage. She was a remarkable woman, and as you can imagine, there were dozens of great vignettes to share about her. The stories he told were "inside" stories that every person in the church knew were true, because they had helped her live them.

His sister-in-law, Julie, was a triathlete. She never smoked or drank, and yet she died young of liver cancer. She was single, and her life focused on her work and her competitions as a triathlete.

In both cases, it was easy to remember the good times and share them with a group of people who came to say goodbye to someone they loved dearly.

But what if you are called on to eulogize someone you did not know so well? Perhaps this is a person you worked with or a parent of a friend or employee. Serving in this role can be far more difficult than eulogizing a relative or loved one. The most difficult eulogy Michael delivered was in 1995 when the father of one of his field agents was suddenly killed in an automobile accident. The mother of this field agent also worked in Michael's agency, and his brother worked for his company in another agency, as did two nephews.

Michael knew the family well, but not intimately. He also knew the deceased well, but not intimately. The family was too grief stricken to perform this task with the impact they wanted, so Michael was asked to serve in this difficult but necessary role.

For over 25 years, Michael had a syndicated column that appeared in many southeastern newspapers and periodicals. He called on his writing experience to interview the surviving sons and their mother, asking the typical *"who, what, when, where, why, how"* kinds of questions. He learned that the deceased, Joe Spinelli, was an educated man. Joe, a successful businessman and father of four children, was quite a competitive person who enjoyed the finer things in life. He was involved in his community and had served in many various civic and fraternal organizations.

Noticeably absent from Michael's remarks were a lot of humorous, first-hand stories. He simply did not know Joe well enough to bring those kind of remarks into the presentation, but it is recommended that you try to, if appropriate, when you are called on to eulogize someone you do not know well.

Following is the eulogy of Joseph J. Spinelli, Sr.:

Today we gather to celebrate the life of Joseph J. Spinelli, Sr. Joe was many things to many people. He was the first child born to George and Marion Spinelli. His gift to them was to carry on their legacy by building one of Florida's finest restaurants. He touched their lives in a special way.

He was a loving brother to Michael and Sandra. He and his wife Diane were loving parents to Jim, George, Sheryl, and Christi. Joe taught his children many things in his 54 years on earth. But perhaps the greatest gift he gave to his children was a work ethic that lives on in each of them. He taught them the value of both a formal education and a "real-world education" as they worked hard in the family business.

He was a wonderful grandfather to Jessica, Joseph, Stephanie, Angela, Tracy, Aaron, and a new baby due on Valentine's Day. He passed his love of fishing on to his children and grandchildren.

He was a caring uncle to Michael and John Spinelli and David and Stephen Shoaff, all of who gather today to act as his pallbearers. He was, indeed, many things to many people.

To his thousands of clients and customers, Joe Spinelli was a man of many talents. After earning his degree in industrial engineering from the University of New Haven, he followed his dream and moved to Florida to go into business for himself. He founded the famous Spinelli Restaurant here in St. Cloud in 1971. He went on to build a second Spinelli's in Melbourne.

Both restaurants were honored many times and in many ways. The *Mobil Travel Guide* accorded Spinelli's a "Four Star" rating. The *Orlando Sentinel* named it the "Best Italian Restaurant in Central Florida." The Florida Restaurant Association called their wine list the best in all of Florida and twice recognized it with its "Most Outstanding Menu Award" in the state of Florida. The *Osceola Gazette* tapped it as the "Best Restaurant in Osceola County." Even the wine cellar at Spinelli's was honored with national telecasts by both ABC and NBC television.

Yes, Joe Spinelli touched many people's lives in many ways. His wife and children learned firsthand the work ethic of this man as they helped him build his successful business.

Joe touched many in the academic community as well. He was a guest lecturer for the American Wine Society. He spoke often at Florida A & M University, the University of Florida Grape Growing Symposium, and the Heublein Management Seminar. He was a frequent guest on numerous television and radio talk shows all over Florida.

Joe was a respected authority on wine making and grape growing. He touched many in that community as well. He was President of the Florida Grape Growers Association. I had the pleasure of delivering the keynote address during his year as president, and I saw firsthand the love and respect that the membership had for him.

As founder of Spinelli Nursery and Spinelli Vineyards, Joe knew firsthand what it took to grow fine grapes and produce excellent wine. He never settled for less than the best from himself or others.

His wines, his fine food creations, and his recipes were subjects of scores of articles and feature stories in local and national publications. Joe himself was a columnist for several central Florida publications on the art of making and enjoying fine wines.

Joe was Chairman of the Viticulture Advisory Council for the State of Florida, which is involved in the study of vines. He received the Wine Spectator Grand Award no less than six times.

Joe and Diane were among only ten restaurant owners in America honored in San Francisco in 1981 with an elegant banquet and dinner, which happened to fall on his 40th birthday. The significance of this award cannot be overstated. In one of the years Joe was honored, he was the only honoree east of the Mississippi selected that year.

In short, Joe Spinelli lived his message. He did not give book reports. The messenger was the message as he touched thousands of people with his knowledge, wit, and charm.

Joe was also actively involved in his community. He was a member of St. Thomas Aquinas Catholic Church here in St. Cloud. He was an active member of the St. Cloud Jaycees and helped form the local chapter. He also served as their first president.

The Honor Guard of the Knights of Columbus Council 6624 gather today to pay homage to one of their own, Brother Knight

Joseph Spinelli. He was a member of the Moose Lodge as well as being an Eagle.

Joe Spinelli believed in giving back to his community and did so repeatedly, often giving free banquets to the Boy Scouts, the Florida Auxiliary Highway Patrol, the St. Cloud Football team, the local educational television station, and countless others.

He served as vice chairman for the Selective Service Board of Osceola, Orange, and Brevard counties. Over the years, his restaurant and wine business donated much to the community and supported it in so many ways.

Joe served on the Grape and Wine Committee for the Florida State Fair. Each year, he hosted the Grape Stomping Festival at Spinelli Farms for hundreds of wine enthusiasts in Central Florida.

Joseph Spinelli looked on life as a banquet and a celebration. He even took up the avocation of flying so he could be present at his son's college football games some 850 miles away from central Florida. Most people lead quiet lives filled with desperation, never quite achieving because they never quite risked. Not Joe Spinelli. In everything he did, Joe lived life to the fullest. He worked hard and he played hard.

Theodore Roosevelt once said, "Far better it is to have dared mighty things, to win glorious triumphs, even though checked by failure . . . than to take rank with those poor spirits who neither enjoy much nor suffer much . . . for they live in a grey twilight that knows not victory nor defeat."

Joe Spinelli lived in the limelight of an active and adventuresome life. He taught his children how to savor life's victories and how to endure its defeats.

The great football coach, Vince Lombardi, once addressed his football team at halftime of a championship game. He said, "It is a reality of life that men are competitive and the most competitive games draw the most competitive men. That is why they are there—to compete. They know the rules and objectives when they get into the game. The objective is to win—fairly, squarely, decently, by the rules . . . but to win! And in truth, I have never known a man worth his salt, who in the long run, deep down in his heart, did not appreciate the grind and the discipline. There is something in good men that really yearns for, that needs, that demands discipline and the harsh reality of head-to-head combat. I do not say these things because I believe in the brute nature of men nor that man must be brutalized to be combative. I believe in God. I believe in human decency. But above all, I believe that any man's finest hour, his greatest fulfillment to all that he holds dear, is that moment when he has worked his heart out in a good cause and lies exhausted on the field of battle . . . victorious." Joe Spinelli was that kind of competitor.

The seventeenth-century poet John Donne once wrote: "No man is an island entire to himself. Every man was a piece of the continent, a part of the main. If a clod be washed away by the sea, Europe is the less, as if its promontory were, as if a manor of thy friends or thine own were. Any man's death diminishes me because I am a part of mankind. And therefore, never send to know for whom the bell tolls. It tolls for thee."

Today, the bell tolled for our friend and loved one, Joseph J. Spinelli, Sr. He is gone, but not forgotten. His life lives on in the hearts and minds of all who gather here today to pay him homage. He was so special in so many ways. Joe, we bid you farewell.

In this eulogy, Michael shared what personal stories he could, but he also drew on some favorite quotes to close it. These were quotes relevant to the deceased, which made them effective.

☞ Master's Tips on Preparing a Eulogy:

- *Learn as much as you can about the deceased.*
- *Interview those close to the deceased.*
- *Find out what they want to remember about the deceased.*
- *Look for a touch of humor along the way, if appropriate.*
- *Accentuate the positive.*
- *Search for appropriate quotes to make your points.*
- *Use the names of those close to the deceased.*
- *Find out what the deceased wanted most to be remembered for.*
- *Tell the deceased's story enthusiastically.*

The Emotional Roller-Coaster Ride of Specialized Presentations

Mastering the skills necessary for effectively delivering these different types of specialized presentations helps make you an invaluable asset to your community. You will also gain a great deal of personal satisfaction knowing that you have the ability to help friends, family, and organizations in their time of need. You'll find some of these presentations fun to do while others are very difficult and necessary. Taking on these challenges helps you grow as a speaker and as a contributing citizen.

***M**aster's Resource Guide*

Bartlett's Familiar Quotations, John Bartlett, Little, Brown.

Braude's Handbook of Stories for Toastmasters and Speakers, Jacob M. Braude, Prentice-Hall.

Dictionary of Quotations, Bergen Evans, Avenel.

The Greatest Speakers I've Ever Heard, Dottie Walters, WRS.

The Harper Dictionary of Modern Thought, Bullock and Stallybrass, Harper-Collins.

High Impact Public Speaking, William T. Brooks, Prentice-Hall.

How to Develop & Promote Successful Seminars & Workshops, Howard L. Shenson, John Wiley & Sons.

The Oxford Dictionary of Quotations, Oxford.

Peter's Quotations, Dr. Lawrence Peter, Morrow.

Secrets of Successful Speakers, Lilly Walters, McGraw-Hill.

Speak and Grow Rich, Dottie Walters, Lilly Walters, Prentice-Hall.

Speaker's Lifetime Library, Leonard and Thelma Spinrad, Prentice-Hall.

Speaking for Money, Gordeon Burgett and Mike Frank, Communications Unlimited, PO Box 1001, Carpinteria, CA 93013.

Spinrads' Encyclopedic Treasury for Speakers, Leonard and Thelma Spinrad, Prentice-Hall.

What to Say When You're Dying on the Platform, Lilly Walters, McGraw-Hill.

$\mathcal{I}$ndex

A

Acceptance speech, 163–65
Acoustics, 152
Acronyms, 150–51
Ad-libbing, 44–45
Adversity, 121–22
Advertising, and quotes, 146
Alcohol consumption, 159
Anecdotes, 25, 153
Announcements, 137–40, 141
Appropriateness, 31, 149, 159
Arch, Dave, 62
Astound!, 91
Audience
    finding, 6–7
    introductions and, 111–12
    participation, 47–63
        approaches to, 47–54
        discussion and roleplaying
            exercises, 56–60
        props and, 60–63
        warm-up exercises, 54–56

seminars and, 133, 134–36
size, and presentation, 67, 144
survey, 48, 50
targeting, 143
Aun, Alice, 169, 170
Aun, Michael, 8
    audience participation and, 58,
        59, 60–62
    eulogies and, 169
    gestures and, 67–68
    humor and, 31, 39–40
    introductions and, 102, 104–5,
        108–12
    motivational speeches and, 122
    preparation and, 72–73
    research by, 24
    seminar selling and, 135, 144
    specialized presentations and,
        160, 161, 164, 169
    topic categories of, 17
    visual aids and, 77, 96
Awareness, creating, 2–3

*A*bout the Authors

Jeff Slutsky, CSP, is a certified professional speaker and author of numerous books on successful marketing. Co-owner of a marketing, advertising, training, and consulting firm, Streetfighter Marketing, he has given hundreds of speeches to companies of all sizes around the world.

Michael A. Aun, FIC, LUTCF, CSP, won "The World Championship of Public Speaking" for Toastmasters International® in 1978. In his capacity as an author, speaker, and general agent for the Knights of Columbus Insurance, Michael makes 150 presentations per year. He holds the prestigious CSP (Certified Speaking Professional), an earned designation of the National Speakers Association, where he has been a member of their board of directors. He has coauthored four books, and his syndicated column has appeared in newspapers and periodicals for a quarter century.

New
CD-ROM Money Maker Kits
from Dearborn Multimedia

Book & CD-ROM Set

A DEARBORN MONEY MAKER KIT

THE MORTGAGE KIT
THIRD EDITION

SELECT THE RIGHT LOAN
NEGOTIATE THE BEST TERMS
LOCK IN THE LOWEST RATE
UNDERSTAND ALL YOUR OPTIONS

THOMAS C. STEINMETZ
PHILLIP WHITT

Features:

- *25 minute video help with the author*
- *12-28 interactive printable forms per CD-ROM*
- *On-Line glossary of terms*
- *Quick-start video tutorial*
- *Interactive printable book on CD-ROM*
  (Print out sections you like for closer reading or writing notes.)

Start Enjoying Greater Financial Freedom
Triple Your Investment Portfolio

SAVE Thousands on Real Estate as a Buyer or Seller

Successfully Start & Manage a NEW Busines

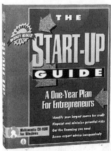